DUBIOUS HONORS

MFK Fisher

NORTH POINT PRESS
SAN FRANCISCO   1988

Grateful acknowledgment is made to the following publishers: Alfred A.
Knopf, Inc. for the preface by M. F. K. Fisher to *Square Meals: A Cookbook*
by Jane and Michael Stern, and for material from *The Physiology of Taste*, *A
Considerable Town*, *As They Were*, and *Sister Age* by M. F. K. Fisher; North
Point Press for the Afterword by M. F. K. Fisher to *The Unprejudiced Palate*
by Angelo Pellegrini, and for material from *Here Let Us Feast*, *Not Now
But* NOW, *A Cordiall Water*, and *Among Friends* by M. F. K. Fisher; The
Macmillan Company for the prefaces to *Serve It Forth*, *The Gastronomical
Me*, *How to Cook a Wolf*, and *An Alphabet for Gourmets* by M. F. K. Fisher;
101 Productions, Inc. for the prefaces to *Pots and Pans, Etc.* by Gertrude
Harris and *The Tea Lover's Treasury* by James Norwood Pratt; Harper &
Row, Publishers for the prefaces to *New American Chefs and Their Recipes*
by Lou Pappas and *The Alice B. Toklas Cook Book* by Alice B. Toklas; Funk
& Wagnalls for the preface to *Cook's and Diner's Dictionary: A Lexicon of
Food, Wine, and Culinary Terms*; Kodansha International for the preface to
Japanese Cooking: A Simple Art by Shizuo Tsuji; Random House, Inc. for
the preface to *Cooking Great Meals Every Day* by Richard Sax and David
Ricketts; University of California Press for the preface to *The Sotheby Book
of California Wine*; The Stephen Greene Press for the preface to *Soup and
Bread: One Hundred Recipes for Bowl and Board* by Julia Older and Steve
Sherman; Andrew Hoyem for the preface to *A Commonplace Book of
Cookery* by Robert Grabhorn; Vintage Books, Inc. for the preface to *Map of
Another Town* from *Two Towns in Provence* by M. F. K. Fisher; and The
Putnam Publishing Group for the preface to *With Bold Knife and Fork* by
M. F. K. Fisher; and The Synergistic Press for the preface by M. F. K.
Fisher to *Not a Station But a Place* by Judith Clancy.

Contents

Dubious Honors

This is a very good way to begin the book, I think: an introduction to all the introductions . . . Suddenly the ranch bell begins to sound Zong! Zong! Zong! quietly, fully, firmly, rung by a young painter who helps the foreman. We ring it every sundown in the summer while David Bouverie is here, and of course on midnight on December 31, even when he's not, to start the new year right. It's always a fine sound, and rolls this way and that, over the valley as the wind moves.

part one

1963

Economy Gastronomy

A GOURMET COOKBOOK
FOR THE BUDGET-MINDED
by SYLVIA VAUGHN THOMPSON

This introduction is to Economy Gastronomy: A Gourmet Cookbook for the
Budget-Minded, *by Sylvia Vaughn Thompson, and has nothing at all to do with
bells. It is the first such thing I ever wrote, just as that book was hers. By now I
can look back on it with some amusement, and with an almost clinical detachment.*

*I find that my prose is rather pedantic, pompous, perhaps evasive, but I am
amused by the whole silly business of starting a so-called collection with this bit,
because it seems impossible to me that it was indeed the first professional thing I
wrote for another person's book, and so long ago. I was asked to do it, I think, or
perhaps I only imagined that Sylvia, a shy beginner, would want me to. And from
the fairly good sale of this book came other nice jobs for her, with mostly good
magazine editors. She wrote better all the time, while she had four fine children.
Then, she took a long professional vacation: she had a rotten bit of luck. In one
of her cookbooks a sentence was left out carelessly, and a kitchen executive or
tester did not as directed punch a hole in a can of condensed milk she was turning
into caramel sauce. The whole thing blew up, of course. The book was taken off*

the market before it was even "out," a real shame . . . and proof positive that all recipes must *be written as if for idiots.*

Sylvia is married to Gene Thompson, also a friend of mine. He keeps her working, which is good. She is vague about her newest book, as of now, but I have talked with her about getting this first one reprinted, because I think it is worth keeping alive and available.

The title, Economy Gastronomy, *seems a little too glib and light. I don't know what she would call this book, the next time around. It is written with much love and with grace. It is a generous book, and it has some little jewels in it. I remember one excellent thing about Caraway Seed Soup. I've never seen it anywhere but in this book, but it has to be one of the most fine-tuned Jewish recipes of all time. (I've made it once, and I thought it was awful, but it would surely cure a cold, as it was meant to!)*

One thing I remember from my first deep reactions to Sylvia's book is how nicely she has always entertained. She loves to cook. She cooks with a steady passion. She loves "doing" a double Bar Mitzvah, a wedding, a celebration, all the cakes, all the cookies, all the traditional dishes. . . .

Another thing I remember that I learned long ago from Sylvia is a wonderful trick about making gingerbread. I could call her basic recipe "Edith's," because my mother gave it to all of us, including Sylvia. Sylvia's invaluable addition, at the end, just before it is poured into the pans, is to fold in a couple or more teaspoons of very finely grated fresh ginger. It makes this into a completely different cake, something "special."

In all these introductions to my introductions, I've decided to forget the possible strictures of inexperience as well as familiarity, and talk with some candor about the hows, the whens, and whys, and even the how muches, if I remember any of these things . . . When, for instance, World published The Art of Eating, *which collects my first five books, they asked Clifton Fadiman to do the introduction. He agreed to, for five hundred dollars, which to me was a strange and awful sum. Apparently it was awful to World, too, because they asked me if I would pay half and that then they would try to pay the other half. I said, "Of course!" (I was innocent and probably rather stupid, that first time so long ago.) But with Sylvia, it never occurred to me to ask for any payment, nor would it now: I was too pleased to have her want me to!*

INTRODUCTION

It sometimes seems to even an amateur observer of the current social scene, gastronomical and otherwise, that there are almost as many cookbooks as there are people to use them. Now and then, however, in the modish flood of "gourmet" hints and hazards, something emerges which is of real value to anyone interested in making it worthwhile to sustain life with grace and fervor . . . to practice the art of eating.

Sylvia Thompson's book seems to me to meet this difficult requirement. It is intelligent, sensitive, and basically practical. It is written by someone who knows what she is doing, both with words and with the "pots and pipkins" of St. Teresa, and who uses them with the same respect.

It is in no sense of the word a pint's-a-pound-the-world-around book. Every good kitchen holds at least one such standby, from Prosper Montagné to Irma Rombauer. They are as necessary as water, even to the deftest cooks.

This book is written with a different ardor, for people who feel as firmly as its author that good cooking can deal as nobly with lamb breast as with ortolans, and with as little apology.

Mrs. Thompson wears her gastronomical enthusiasm like shining armor, a dedicated apostle of the Tenth Muse, and while she is dead-serious about cookery as such, she happily misses making it either solemn or pompous.

She cooks the way some people play the stock market, or go to their analysts, or design sports cars. For her the construction of a simple but fastidious meal is a game of wits, and it is spiritual therapy, and it is as functional as speed itself.

This dedication to an art is not at all obsessive in Mrs. Thompson, but it is an expression of her sensitive realization that since we must eat to live, we can be better humans for doing so with grace and love. Indeed, her whole book is a kind of hymn, never noisy but always sung with a true pitch, to the power of kindness . . . at table as everywhere else.

The fact that her book is written to make such harmony possible to the thinnest purses has nothing to do with stinginess or suspicion of extravagance or any of the other cardinal sins of gastronomy. She is experienced, not only in the art of cooking, but in the equally taxing art of how to behave with the most balance and poise, both at table and in her other relationships with the people she loves and nourishes.

The recipes set forth in this book are tried-and-true, perfected with long practice, and written with a rare appreciation of the values of natural flavor and texture and of full enjoyment. Some of them are rare. All of them are worth the time and thought that make their basic value. They can and do serve as a kind of aesthetic reassurance, in this day of TV Dinners and All-Purpose Pills, that young and vital American women still find time, whether or not it be for therapeutic and/or amorous reasons, to bolster their aims in life with a stew or a delicate dumpling or a lightly scrambled egg.

One proof of the appeal of this cookery book of Mrs. Thompson's is that while it is written from a completely female point of view, almost a love song to the powers of satisfaction, it is eminently appealing to the fine cook who hides in most males.

The intricacies of seasoning, never affected but always essential; the fussy testing and timing; the ritual of assembling and brewing and tasting; finally the dramatic serving forth: all these are grist to the mill of any yearning kitchen artist, of no matter what age and sex but especially to the man who has thus far been pushed pityingly onto the patio, to grill a steak and roast six potatoes in aluminum foil.

It has been said that senseless economy is a great extravagance. In the recipes that Mrs. Thompson gives here in loving detail, there is, in spite of the inexpensive meats and fruits and vegetables from which they are made, a rare generosity of spirit as well as skill. A true enjoyment of one of our basic necessities can never be anything but dust in our mouths and acid in our bodies, without such compassion and selflessness to season it.

Experience and skill show everywhere in this cookery book, but the essence of it is its basic recognition that the ritual of preparing good food for good people makes them better. It gives courage to them, and to the cook too. . . .

1965

Napa Wine

A CHAPTER FROM
"THE SILVERADO SQUATTERS"
by ROBERT LOUIS STEVENSON

The next time I wrote an introduction, I felt that being asked *to do it was the first real compliment of my life. It was paid me by Jim Beard—James E. Beard. He was a fine printer, a tall skinny man of St. Helena. He died near Christmas, in 1984, within a day or two of tall fat James A. Beard's death. I loved both those men very much. They were completely different, in every way.*

I remember James E. Beard would say, "Who the hell is this fellow, James A.? I get his mail now and then, and it's a damned nuisance! Who is he?" I would say, "You'd like him;" and he'd snarl, "Never! Not on your life!" But one time James A. Beard—Fat Jim—was coming out from New York to have dinner and stay overnight with Robert Mondavi and his wife, and they asked the St. Helena Beards and me to dinner too.

I told the Mondavis about this firm idea of Jim's that he was never going to meet "that bastard." They laughed, and had an especially nice family dinner, of course very Italian. The two Mondavi boys were there with a wife and a girlfriend. I remember their mother went out to the kitchen with the cook, and then came into the living room with a little bowl of soup, for Bob to taste before it was served.

It was somewhat affected, too "peasant," but still openly amabile. *I loved that. And, in the same Italian style, which seemed heavy and still "right" for that night, there was a long grace by Bob, before we all ate. Then there was another long grace after dinner! But it was not embarrassing, and James A. and James E. liked each other at* once. *We all felt happy.*

"Skinny Jim" of St. Helena, in about 1963 or 1964, began to print a little book called Napa Wine: A Chapter from "The Silverado Squatters," *by* Robert Louis Stevenson. *It was copyrighted in 1965. He asked me to write the introduction. I don't know why, except that he liked me, and he knew that I was a writer.*

I never much cared for Robert Louis Stevenson's essays, so sedately stylized they seemed almost archaic, but of course I was raised on Treasure Island, *and everything else he ever wrote. And I considered it a great honor to be asked by Jim, who was a master printer, to add to his book. I worked hard, did a lot of good research, and loved the whole project. My only embarrassment was that we had to cut my piece down a lot, because it was longer than Stevenson's chapter!*

Jim gave me three copies of the book from his limited printing. He printed two hundred copies, I think, that sold for $7.50, but by now it fetches much more for the first handsewn copies (copies of that are still for sale at the Schramsberg Winery in Calistoga). I helped bind it, and I learned how to make signatures. Jim and his wife, Yolande, and I did it at night . . . two nights, three or four, in their remodeled barn. It was fun. Most of that time was very good.

The book is a beautiful little job. I'm proud of that, and of course of Jim, James E. Beard. (And the other Jim, too!)

INTRODUCTION

Robert Louis Balfour Stevenson lived only forty-four years from his birth in Edinburgh in 1850, but his life was one of the most troubled and romantic and joyful of his century. In what his friend Edmund Gosse called his "hurrying and painful pilgrimage" (from Scotland through Europe, across America, back to Europe and then, after one last search in New York State for health and strength, throughout the South Seas until he died among the Samoans who had named him their beloved chief), he stopped for a few poignant and enchanted months in the Northern California valley named Napa by its vanished Indians.

This was in 1880. He was deeply in love with "a certain Mrs. Osbourne," as his disapproving family said until they finally met her, and he was at last married to her after a long and socially shocking courtship. (Fanny was an American divorcée with two children; he was a doomed invalid, ten years younger than she, and habitually penniless. . . .)

The Stevensons moved into one of the desolate buildings of a deserted silver-mining camp, part way up Mount St. Helena, which looms, mysterious and cool after its volcanic birth, at the north end of the rich narrow slopes of Napa Valley. Fanny's sturdy devotion kept them clean and nourished and always hospitable, and Lou Stevenson roamed with new vigor along the trails and roads of the boom-town activity of the mines, and lived warmly with his bride, and wrote letters that glowed with enthusiasm through their skilled phraseology.

These were metamorphosed, as so often happens with good spontaneous prose, into *The Silverado Squatters*, from which this one chapter called "Napa Wine" is taken. The book was published in 1883, when the Stevensons were once more wandering in their unquiet search for his health, this time to Hyères in the south of France.

By then he was recognized as one of the most graceful and vital writers of his time, and the romantic simplicity of the new book excited readers wherever English was read. The first editors of *The Silverado Squatters*, however, decided that even such a brief discussion of Napa wines as the one herein printed would hold little interest, except perhaps to London club-stewards willing to stock exotic bottles from the Far Wild West, and the whole chapter was omitted when the revised letters first appeared.

Stevenson's rather dismal introduction to this excerpt from the definitive edition of the book was obviously written in Hyères. Perhaps he had been talking with temporarily depressed vintners of that region. Perhaps he had been reading gloomy reports from Bordeaux and Burgundy. (Wine men, like all farmers, are inclined both vocally and in print to take a dim view of even such friendly enemies as the sun and moon. . . .) Whatever the reason, Stevenson felt a clear nostalgia for the brash but solid young wines of far-away Napa Valley, as he sat waiting under the palm trees of southern France for the strong health that never came. His tongue once more tasted what he had recognized as the "smack of Californian earth" in Jacob Schram's cellar-cool bottles, and his homesick ears heard again the music of his native Scots, that summer afternoon in 1880 when he and Fanny stopped at Colin McEachran's cottage on the road up to Schramsberg.

The road is still there. The thimbleberries and the buckeyes still bloom along it in their green dusty tangle. The ex–sea captain McEachran's "little bit of a wooden house" and his "patch of vines" are gone, but the old Schram place still rides its wide verandas, and the dim deep tunnel of a cellar where Stevenson tasted the German barber's meticulously tended vintages still holds its just share of bottles.

That cellar is now a historical monument, so marked by the State. It has seen good and bad days. It is, hopefully, indestructible. Its fame is surely so, for what Stevenson wrote about it in "Napa Wine" keeps forever the feel, the sense, of its first dedication to the making and then the drinking of its "bottled poetry."

After Jacob Schram, with native practicability, dug into the cool mountainside for proper storage for his wines, using the Chinese labor so easily come by in the 1860s in Napa Valley, some of his knowing colleagues did the same, and now there are other eerie caverns lined with casks and bottles along the slopes, but none so old as his.

There, that fine day nearly a century ago, the short jolly German and the tall, thin, vividly attractive Scot tasted well and slowly a good round of bottles that still live on our palates in Stevenson's listing: "every variety and shade of Schramberger, red and white . . . Burgundy . . . Hock . . . Golden Chasselas . . . and I fear to think how many more."

Up on the veranda, where stuffed birds stood elegantly about, the two wives chatted of far places they both knew, above the dwindling voice of the little canyon stream, which still rushes when the time is right. Below, on the rough bosky road that follows it, the dignified bachelor McEachran savored the earlier visit of his countryman (Stevenson wrote his name as it was said in their own tongue: M'Eckron. Quite probably the visitors saluted him again as they went down into the valley, but no mention was ever made of his wine itself, and by now even the memory of his little Alta Vineyard is vague. . . .)

When Captain McEachran was very old, in about 1897, he answered some queries about the famous visit in a slow trembling left hand, because his right one had failed him. ". . . [Stevenson] was very enthusiastic," he noted firmly, "as to the future prosperity of this section of the country, particularly as a producer of wine."

Robert Louis Stevenson had indeed felt an unquestioning enthusiasm that fine afternoon in 1880, and then recalled it with innate confidence, the later gloomier day on a hill above the Mediterranean. The wines of Napa Valley, for him then as for us now, had yielded their "inimitable fragrance and soft fire."

"They bide their hour," he wrote. He called them "blood and sun," as much a child of Nature as Man himself. He looked from the vineyards of the Old World, staggering with desuetude and on-creeping disease, to the new plantings of America and Australia, and he felt cheered. And his vigorous acceptance of this constant change in the world's wines, as in men, is alive and cheering still, in this small view of what he saw and tasted, one early summer day near Calistoga, in the Napa Valley.

1968

Cook's & Diner's Dictionary
A LEXICON OF FOOD, WINE,
AND CULINARY TERMS

In 1968 I wrote an introduction to a book published by Funk & Wagnalls, called Cook's & Diner's Dictionary: A Lexicon of Food, Wine, and Culinary Terms. *I did it for Sam Davis, a firm good friend. He wrote to me about the job because he liked things that I had written, and it was very easy: I simply went on and on about dictionaries, which I have always loved.*

I see references on the first page to "my Curious Nose" and André Simon's Encyclopedia of Gastronomy . . . *and* The Oxford English Dictionary . . . *and then C. T. Onions . . . and so forth. I seem to have done plenty of research!*

The book itself was not at all as extensive or intensive or long or authoritative as it should have been, and it fell on deaf ears, and partly deservedly. I never did ask Sam about it, but I don't think it sold at all well, and the whole thing was probably dismissed as a real flop. As far as I know, nobody got even a fan letter about it.

The best part about this whole bookish fiasco was that I met Sam Davis and his friend Ron in New York one time, I think after I wrote the introduction. They lived in a posh, starkly furnished apartment, with a big view of the East River.

They gave me one of the most thoughtful and generous and nice dinners I've ever had. The light was beautiful on the polished floors, and we sat for a long time without any electricity or candles. We drank quite a lot of good dry champagne and there was black caviar. The two men were very quiet, but it was so friendly that I felt both shy and extremely glamorous. Finally one of them took me in a cab to the other part of town, miles away, where I was staying on West 12th Street.

And later, they sent me a beautiful piece of Greek weaving that they'd found on one of the smaller islands. It had been worn once every hundred years by the queen of the cooks of that island, and although it is probably one of the oldest artifacts I have ever owned, it looks barely worn. It is a beautiful soft reddish thing that looks more Oriental than Greek or even Guatemalan, and it's had a new fringe put on parts of it so that there are bits of silk in it that are a modern color like "shocking pink." Sam and Ron told me that it was the oldest piece of Greek weaving they had ever seen. I see it every day, hanging on a wall here.

It seems strange that I'll probably never see either of these men again. Sam telephones now and then from a little town in Pennsylvania where he runs the college bookstore, and I always feel better after we've talked, as if we were much more important to each other than even we would assume. He writes a good letter, rarely, and I write back but seldom, and someday I may read the Dictionary *and even its introduction, but I doubt it.*

P.S. And in 1974 or 1975, I found that Poutargue was served in the Hôtel de France in Aix. It was almost an exotic, a curiosity, then and there. The chef told me that nobody liked it anyway, but he put it on his menu for the tourists. I agreed with him, and with the descriptions I'd first looked up for Botargo!

Introduction

A dictionary is in its simplest sense a word-book. It is a list in alphabetical order of the words of a language, with their meanings and usages. It tries, in the clearest and briefest possible ways, to give the significance of sounds which people of one race or nation or even region make over and over again in the same way.

To do this, other words must be used! It is a circle which need not be vicious, but which is hard to keep small, as any lexicographer will admit. A classic and awesome example is *The Oxford English Dictionary on Historical Principles*, which between 1884 and 1928 was published in twenty half-volumes, numbering 15,000 large quarto pages, compiled by hundreds of editors all over the world. Fortunately for people like me, with a Curious Nose but limited space and funds, a smaller edition was compiled, a most delicate job of surgical abridgement performed by C. T. Onions and a skilled staff. (One I feel a special empathy for: "Mrs. E. A. Coulson . . . responsible for W." I hope she has descendants who sometimes boast of her with just that phrase. . . .)

I like to say a word, any word, to myself, and then for amusement to read about it in my surprisingly worn edition: *caviar*, for instance. I am personally acquainted with caviar, to my lasting joy and whether in actuality or on the mind's tongue. But now I also know that Dean Swift wrote of it in a jingle like this: ". . . And for our home-bred English Cheer, / Botargo, Catsup, and Caveer." So I must find what I can about Botargo, since I feel myself safe with Caveer and on fairly sure ground with Catsup (tomato, mushroom, walnut, et al). Naturally it is not in any ordinary word-book, but it is in an old Funk & Wagnalls' Unabridged, where it is defined as "A thirst-provoking relish much used on the Mediterranean coast, made of the salted roe of mullet, tunny, Russian sturgeon, and other fishes." By the time it turned up in England in 1598 (How? Why?) it was a relish or appetizer, made of the roe of the mullet or tunny, and somewhere in his journal Samuel Pepys wrote of it, "Drinking great drafts of claret, and eating botargo, and bread and butter."

Here my Curious Nose gets the better of my good intention to work and not play, and I find in André Simon's *Concise Encyclopedia of Gastronomy* that Botargo is still the Italian name of the salted roe of both gray mullet and tunny, and is known in France as *Boutargue* or *Poutargue*. A little signal sounds faintly, but in spite of it I must sniff further for words under B . . . and I find neither Botargo nor Boutargue in several French kitchen manuals of varying worth. I choose to give my mind the word from the Italian. It sounds better . . . except for that signal coming from somewhere. . . .

A regular standard dictionary is perhaps not as diverting as Simon's, but it is still a bedside companion for many a semantical insomniac, and it can always turn me from a dull task if I let myself pick up one of the small-sized editions I seem to scatter about the house as some people do ashtrays.

They tend to drift homeward when children move from high school to college to marriage to general war-and-peace. This minute, for instance, in order to put off walking to the post office until it is too late for the noon mail, which perversely I want to miss, I can look up another word in Simon. Why not *garum*?

Garum, of course: the salty rotting juices of fish-innards laid in the sun with spices and wines, to make a sauce for the rapidly putrefying Roman Empire . . . and to shape the path for our own ubiquitous "Worcestershire"! Good old garum! Its blunt directive has titillated many an armchair gastronomer, since it was first written about 400 B.C. I reach to read it again. In spite of my brave attempt to abstain, I need one more for the road, one quick nip before the bottle is snatched from me. But instead I steal a sniff at what I fear is an empty glass . . . and there at the bottom, like half a forgotten swallow, is a recipe for Poutargues! I *knew* I had heard the word somewhere, although Simon's *Concise* is a long way from Marseille! And in *La Cuisinière Provençale*, by J. B. Reboul, it stands as plain as fish and salt among the Salted Fish he discusses in his little beauty of a regional cookbook (which is still to be found in Aix and Arles and Avignon).

A poutargue, which I think I have not eaten and perhaps not even seen, is the whole roe of a mullet (*Poutargo de mufou* in Mistral's sweet language) which has been salted, pressed, and then dried. It sounds like a kind of marine jerky. It sounds tough, fishy, salty, and smelly. I do not hunger actively for it, but it is satisfying that I have found it, semantically at least . . . and by now it is far too late to make the noon mail. . . .

This somewhat devious exposure of the dangers of word-sniffing may be proof positive that it is an addiction, like glue- or snow-sniffing in a somewhat less destructive way, physically if not economically. (It would be very hard for me to concentrate on writing an introduction, for instance, or even a dictionary, if I were any more surrounded by them.) As an addict, however, I am almost guiltily interested in converts to my own illness, and in a pinch I can recommend nearly any reasonable solace, whether or not it qualifies as a true descendant of Noah Webster.

There are other word-books which for personal reasons stand on higher steps of my mind's ladder. Probably the favorite, although not of infallible balance, is one printed on India paper which I really dislike using because it is so flimsy, and repaired at least twice, drastically, since it was given to me when I was going on seventeen. It was first bound in elegant leather of a donnish dark blue, with discreet gold lettering on the spine. It bit into my heart as well as my mind, for part of me was flattered almost unbearably to be given such an intellectual prop by my favorite male cousin, and another part was rocked back for decades because to my younger sister he gave a bottle of French perfume. I felt that a message had been delivered to me, by my cousin and other gods: I was a bluestocking, the kind of female men never kiss-and-all-that. It was a mixed awakening, certainly, a declared conflict between superego and plain id which fortunately was fought later on other grounds. But the little dictionary has gone everywhere with me, through wars of all kinds and shapes and colors, and now in its third restoration (green buckram, no lettering) stands within reach, for quick assurance.

It is an interesting game to decide for oneself where a dictionary ends and an encyclopedia begins. Technically there is a clear difference: an encyclopedia can discuss a word, and at times ramble for pages about its description, history, and so on, where a dictionary must state as briefly as possible what it should mean in the language it belongs to. A good case in point, perhaps, is this present book of culinary words and terms in comparison with *Larousse Gastronomique*, or better yet the quirky and entertaining *Concise Encyclopedia of Gastronomy*. Correctly, the Larousse is what it calls itself, an "encyclopedia of food, wine, and cookery," giving the origins of a word or term, some of its history, and then most often explaining one or several ways to make what it is: a certain kind of cake, a sauce. It is also a dictionary, somewhat wordier than "concise," and it describes exactly what *is* a mushroom or a giblet, or a custard cup. Simon's lexicon, on the other hand, is called an encyclopedia, but in many ways is more a dictionary, as when it says for *Pampano*, for instance, "See Pompano," a frustratingly familiar pattern for word buffs in any language. This new culinary lexicon, the *Cook's and Diner's Dictionary*, has tried, with overall success, to stay clearly on the classical side of the fence, semantically, and say what *mulligatawny* is, for example, giving its pronunciation and its origins in the Tamil language but without going into the exact proportions of curry, stock, chicken, coconut, etc., necessary to make this peculiar and delicious East Indian soup.

Not too long ago it was believed that one mind, or a couple of them, could perform such a fantastic feat as to produce a lexicon. Now dozens and even hundreds of people work on one book, and I have no idea of the number of amateur and professional word-sleuths who have contributed to this new collection of names and terms. I have never worked on such a project, myself, but I should think the most painful part of it would be deciding when to stop, when to close the door upon the changes that must inevitably happen the next day, or next week, to a meaning or even a pronunciation.

Noah Webster did a monumental job of presenting our American language to skeptical speakers of English, in 1828, and in England, some seventy-five years earlier, Samuel Johnson's *Dictionary* was first published in two folio volumes. Even though it was admittedly inadequate from its beginning, his personal claim to literary greatness was so firm that it influenced lexicography for a long time. Its 2,300 pages would fill about ten modern volumes, and Johnson worked alone on it from 1746 until 1755, reading every kind of printed authority on every subject his amazing mind could ponder. Of course he fed his material to helpers, to be checked and copied, but the book was his in every sense, and it remains an astonishingly clear and exciting portrait not only of the language and thought of his time, but of the man himself. (It is fortunate for people like me that a small and tasteful "selection" has been brought out in the past decade, to make available his Preface and a goodly sampling of his definitions.)

Johnson's dictionary is opinionated, pithy, and vigorous. Personal grief hides in some words in Latin or Greek, with touching scholarly discretion; there are few overt political taunts, considering the man's sardonic nature; there is smooth erudition, but common slangy words are noted with the same serious courtesy, although he did not hold with obscenity as such. Perhaps most endearing of all, he was not afraid to admit to lapses in his near-encyclopedic knowledge, and in his Preface he wrote, "Some words there are which I cannot explain, because I do not understand them."

His own definition of a writer of dictionaries was "a harmless drudge," and he classed himself in his long task as one of those "unhappy mortals" condemned to the endless and futile job of keeping ahead of any language in flux. This was, he felt, to pursue perfection, like "the first inhabitants of Arcadia, to chace the sun, which, when they had reached the hill where he seemed to rest, was still beheld at the same distance from them."

Happily, neither Johnson nor his disciples could be muffled by his bluntly fatalistic opinion, and along with the unceasing flow of gazetteers, indexes, concordances, and other types of lexicons in our language, there is now this kitchen vocabulary, a "lexicon of food, wine, and culinary terms." I need it. I shall use it. Surely I'll reach for it sometime and not find in it the word I hunt, just as I can do with any of my dictionaries, even Johnson. Surely I'll disagree with an accent or a pronunciation mark, now and then. But in the main I'll feel content to know that there among the sternly limited books which I call essential in my kitchen library I can find, if I wish to, a clear, short, and correct definition of, for instance, a plum, an Edam cheese, a capon, and that it will be properly plum, *not* Plum—not edam cheese, Capon!

I may think that I know what each of these is, but it is fun now and then to endanger my own smugness, and to obey my Curious Nose and sniff out possible newness in old tricks. And then, inevitably, I am tempted to risk missing the noon mail again and take a quick look into another word-book. I'll choose something like *Eel* in my new lexicon and in one or two others, to amuse myself and cheat the clock. An eel, I first read here, is "a long, snake-like fish . . . flesh somewhat fat and heavy . . . can be cooked in any number of interesting ways . . . considered real delicacy, especially by European gourmets . . . delicious smoked!" Avoiding the quaint attraction of Simon's book, I go straight to Johnson's, and he dismisses the word in a curtly nongastronomical way: "A serpentine slimy fish, that lurks in mud."

In some justification of this semantic shrug, I go on quickly, to find his much-quoted definition of *oats*: "A grain, which in England is generally given to horses, but in Scotland supports the people." He is usually credited with a chauvinistic sneer in this quasi-sentence, but it is most probably no more than plain truth, set down by a "harmless drudge," which the wittiest of men would sometimes be at such a mighty task as the Doctor's. I sniff on happily, after this protective little gesture toward one of my favorite people, and a tiny etymological tidbit falls into its right place, with the great man's definition of "garous. Resembling pickle made of fish." Of course! *Garum* again, one of my verbal touchstones! I never saw the word garous before, but now I know it is a good and fairly ancient adjective, straight from London and Rome, *old* Rome, to describe something that stinks of rotting fish and sour wine. . . .

There are many words in the *Cook's and Diner's Dictionary* which were unborn in 1755: dip, barbecue, baked Alaska . . . and there is no mention in it or in Johnson's of Botargo, by now almost tangibly on my mind's tongue. (I am already inclined to refer to it as Poutargue, because I am at least half in Provence anyway, in mind or heart. . . .) Johnson does not mention caviar, even as caveer, but he does give a fine if somewhat casual definition of *custard*, which I cannot match in the new book: "A kind of sweetmeat made by boiling eggs with milk and sugar, 'till the whole thickens into a mass. It is a food much used in city feasts.

> He cram'd them 'till their guts did ake,
> With cawdle, *custard*, and plumb cake.
>   *Hudibras*, Cant. ii."

Here I am of course honor-bound to see if I am right, that a caudle is something connected with tripe or sausage meat. I am not right. I am indeed completely mistaken. My new word-book says *caudle* is "A hot drink, popular with the elderly and invalid, especially in England of another day. It consists of ale or wine (or, for teetotalers, tea), gruel, eggs, sugar, and spices. In the hospitals and on the great estates, it was made in rather large amounts in a cauldron because it was served not only to the ill but to their visitors as well."

When I was being raised in a word-loving family near Los Angeles, a couple of centuries after Johnson's dictionary, we kept an *Unabridged* on a hideous wrought-iron pedestal in a corner of the dining room. The volume was enormous, too big for any of us children to lift or even to read without standing on a little stool when we first learned to use it, and it was as natural a part of the furniture as the corner cupboard with the Belleek tea-set behind its glass doors. Our family talked a lot at table, and only two subjects were taboo: politics and personal troubles. The first was sternly avoided because Father ran a nonpartisan daily in a small town, with some success, and did not wish to express his own opinions in public, even when in private. The second one included worries about money, illness, feuds, and general ill-nature. Surprisingly enough, these fences still left us wide fields, and we managed to express ourselves with increasing deftness as we trotted from the table to the dictionary and back, according to our capabilities and our inner convictions.

"When in doubt, consult the dictionary," was standard at meals, and the person who had used a word questionably, or the oldest child (which I usually seemed to be), would not need to hear more than the beginning of the phrase from either parental end of the table before getting up obediently (if with a raging heart and stomach) to find the meaning of anything from *ass* to *zounds* . . . all read in a clear firm voice, of course. And the talk would go on.

That worn and bulky volume did not survive its move from the corner of the dining room, when my family split into its many logical or at least irrevocable parts, and the iron stand, by now a collector's modish dream, has disappeared instead of simply disintegrating. All of our new houses are well stocked with the smaller duller dictionaries we can buy even in paperbacks today, and new batches of children still consult them, when in doubt or, as with me too, in a playful or anxious or even dawdling mood. Perhaps this type of addiction is congenital?

Just as it was mysteriously satisfying to have Samuel Johnson present me with an eighteenth-century adjective which I *know* must come from one of my familiars, the Roman *garum*, so it is to wander, lazy but still alert for odd clues, from his all-encompassing lexicon to this current culinary vocabulary, which is perforce limited by its subject, whereas he wrote definitions of mankind itself. Here, for instance, and for no reason except that it is on a page waiting for me, is the word *farce*. In my new book it is the French name for the "stuffing" for meat, fowl, or vegetables, made with garlic and herbs, or ham and mushrooms, or pork or veal or countless other things, depending upon its purpose and its envelope. Dr. Johnson puts it as "A dramatick representation, written without regularity and stuffed with wild and ludicrous conceit."

Of course! Even a novice at the stove will recognize a masterly description of at least half of the farces served forth, stuffed too often with wild and ludicrous flavors and assembled without stern obedience to a master-plan, whether by Escoffier or Euripides. There is an immediate and obvious connection between the stage game and the culinary one. Discipline is essential to both, even with wild and ludicrous conceits, but "The Taming of the Shrew" is never "Charlie's Aunt," any more than Carême's recipe for Truffle Stuffing for a Turkey is Cousin Maggie's Corn-pone Mixture. These turn out all right, in their strict or zany ways, because there is what Johnson calls "regularity" in them, whereas a careless slapstick effort in either theater or kitchen will go almost at once into merciful if dyspeptic oblivion. There are a lot of plays on my shelves. So are Carême and Escoffier, and in my cooking-file the corn-pone recipe. And along with them and all their fellows, to add to my pleasures and at times my moral strength, are Johnson's dictionary and this new one. When in doubt, I shall consult them, for any of a dozen reasons. . . .

Pots & Pans, Etc.
by GERTRUDE HARRIS

In 1971 I wrote an introduction to Pots & Pans, Etc. *by Gertrude Harris published by 101 Productions in San Francisco. At first, it was a funny little book published in a tall thin format. Later it was enlarged to a more normal size, but it was always about pots and pans, no more. Gertrude Harris is a strange tidy little woman. She lives now in San Francisco, but for a long time lived on Point Richmond in San Francisco Bay, when there were beautiful eucalyptus trees and little patches of lovely land everywhere. Now it is mostly great tanks of oil . . .*

Gertrude was married for a long time to an Italian artist. He lived in Rome and she out here, and she spoke good Italian. Once she went to China, and when she came home she had adopted the long dark dress of the Chinese women, and she looked like a tiny little square on feet, about four-by-five. She is delightful. I don't think I ever got any payment for my work, and certainly not from her, but why should I? It was fun to do. I learned a lot about aluminum and tin and iron. And what is best, I met a friend.

PREFACE

It has often been told us, in one form or another, that it is easier to lie some-times than to tell the truth. I have never found this so: I have been acutely miserable in my few attempts to prove the theory, and that is why I feel very comfortable in stating what is for me a plain fact about Gertrude Harris's little jewel of a book, *Pots & Pans, Etc.*

It is a jewel.

Thanks to it I now count the writer as a friend, but long before I had met her, and only shortly after I had read the book, I wrote her one of the two or three fan letters of my life, with sincere thanks for what she had done. That was about four years ago, I think. Now there is this new edition, and it is even more of a Kitchen Friend than the first one, if that be possible.

Near my stove there is a short shelf of books that are *needed*, any time of day or night, so *P&P, Etc.* is always close to hand. I buy a new heavy-gauge aluminum saucepan (which I do every thirty years or so), or somebody gives me a cast-iron soup kettle for my Franklin stove (once in a lifetime!), or I decide to use stainless-steel spoons (which I did lately). I reach for my little paperback, and go ahead confidently with the new acquisitions. And all the time I wonder where else on God's green earth I could find such help, except in this book. . . .

The main trouble with it is that after I have let it answer my current question, I go on reading what else Harris has to say on momentarily irrel-evant subjects, except of course that they are all about cooking tools. I smile, for instance, at her obvious aesthetic enjoyment of two large brass pans she bought, from Hong Kong: "Although the metal is fairly thin, the rims of both pan and lid are cleverly worked into a beaded edge to give the pan sturdiness and solidity. The lid fits firmly into a 'ditch' formed by the beaded edge, which also prevents condensed moisture from escaping down the sides of the pan. The design and handcraft . . . triumph over the disadvantages of the thin metal."

This description is eminently practical, but it reveals a kind of empathy with the subject of what St. Teresa called her "pots and pipkins" that subtly enlivens the whole straightforward treatise.

Nothing could be more candid than Harris's advice on the care and usage of materials. In the chapter on porcelain and enamelware, she writes of the latter: "If food has stuck or burned on, soaking with a little soapy water to which a little ammonia is added, should take care of it. If a roaster, used in high oven heats, has a stubborn stain or foods stuck to it, I sometimes spray on a little 'window cleaner' (the kind with ammonia added), and leave it on for a while. It seems to do the trick." The whole small book is unadorned by fancy language, but it has real style, and now and then a wry or subtle joke may be left dangling for the wary reader . . . *only* if it will not mislead anyone, of course. And there is a continuing feeling that the author knows by both instinct and training what she discusses, as when she says casually, "It is well known that a chef's knife, like a cowboy's pony, will not permit a stranger to ride it."

And the research behind all this seemingly modest and casual guide to kitchenware is awesome, to my mind. There is the index, of course, an excellent one. There are the fascinating sections at the back: The Cooking Utensils Questionnaire, Terminology . . . they are intelligent, thoughtful, almost prescient to anyone like me. And then there are chapters like the one about aluminum and its care, which also asks if it is "safe," and quotes varied nutritional authorities, straight-faced and honest as all get-out, about the yeses and the nos. (Choose your poison, as the old bartenders used to say . . . but Harris is both fair and reassuring.)

Perhaps the most important chapter is called, in a typically matter-of-fact way, "How to Beat the System." Personally I would simplify that to Good Advice, except that the whole book is good advice and there is no need to call it *A Book of Good Advice About Pots & Pans, Etc.* . . . . except that it is exactly that!

At the risk of sounding either hired, which I am not, or moonstruck, which I have not been for several decades, I shall try to be as plain and sensible as the prose I am discussing, and make a flat statement that I think this book should be given to every child of ten if bright and of twelve if somewhat retarded. It should be kept on hand, straight through high school (chemistry classes, etc.: metals . . . alloys . . . acids . . .) and on into inevitable connubial complications, many of which focus as much in the kitchen as in the bedroom. And once consulted . . . the burned skillet, the new egg-poacher . . . it will remain close by, neat in design and format, and clear in its wisdom.

It is indeed a jewel.

1972

My Paris
by MAURICE CHEVALIER

In 1972 I wrote a foreword to My Paris *by Maurice Chevalier. First, though, I translated the whole book because my friend Eleanor Friede was publishing it for Macmillan and we both thought it would be a jolly little prank, almost, for me to do it. I had already written a translation of another book by a Frenchman, Brillat-Savarin. He was an erudite and sophisticated man of Gaul, and a good old man too. Mr. Chevalier, being a Frenchman too, was also sophisticated and perhaps good, and certainly old, but it was equally certain that he was not erudite!*

Of course, I admired Maurice Chevalier very much as a performer. He wrote well, too, and in a straightforward simple fashion that Brillat-Savarin would have admired. And he was appalled, absolutely appalled, when he read my trans-lation. It was not at all what he wanted or expected. He was a famous performer and a consummate music-hall artiste, and he expected me to write what he thought his American public wanted him to sound like. I should have been very "ooh-la-la." I should have somehow written as Miss America thought Maurice Chevalier should sound—all "zats" and "zoses." In other words, I should have rewritten everything that he had done in French into a kind of Yankee version of "Voulez-vous coucher avec moi?"

Chevalier's French was so honest and straight and clear that I could not possibly distort it. I was distressed, and my dear friend Eleanor said, "There is just one thing we can do." I said, "Yes, let's forget the whole thing." She said, "Maybe, but first he's going to pay you for doing all this work, because he's a rude old man." Of course, the poor spoiled grumpy fellow did hate my translation. Why should he pay me for something he didn't like? But Eleanor said, "Nonsense. You're going to be paid $1,000, and he is going to print a letter from you at the beginning of this book, and then he can go find himself another translator." And she added, "That will be very easy . . . there are plenty of people who can write the silly stuff he wants. But your letter will be a lesson to him and to them . . ."

And so she did as she planned: I wrote to Chevalier, in 1972, and she printed the letter at the beginning of the otherwise somewhat less distinguished prose (as she and I both like to think), and it turned into a collection of superb photographs by Robert Doisneau and otherwise was a complete flop. I honestly think that if I'd been allowed to translate it as literally as I did Brillat-Savarin, a word-for-word job, it might be alive today, for his good prose as well as Doisneau's fine pictures.

The letter I wrote is sentimental, but I liked it. It was no less truthful than his own writing had seemed to me, and I'm very glad that everything happened just as it did.

P.S. Eleanor and Maurice paid me $1,000. He did it so that I would not translate him; and she did it for a love letter that I would have written anyway if I'd had the nerve. And perhaps I should add that I wrote the letter before I got the lucre, which proves that money is not really what makes the world go 'round.

FOREWORD

Dear Mr. Chevalier:
Beloved charming delightful Maurice:
Either way of addressing you is correct in my private Book of Behavior, for I respect you very much and I have also been in love with you since early in

1929, when I skipped college classes several times to educate myself, no matter how vicariously, in a movie house in Pasadena, California, where your first or at least my first American Chevalier was showing. (You sang "Louise.")

Then in the natural progression of an unrequited but still undying *affaire*, I found myself working one or two decades later in Hollywood, and I passed you in the hall of the Writers' Building at Paramount. That was too long ago for precise remembering, but it is certain that my scalp prickled and my heart quickened its beat before it seemed to pause a little. I would have liked to stop you in your starry tracks, but there was nothing to say to you except "*Oh*, Mr. Chevalier!"

The years went on, of course. One day when I was living in Aix-en-Provence I arranged to take my two young daughters and three even younger visiting nephews to Cassis. I had known it as an unfashionable tiny port long before the Second World War and had shunned revisiting it, not liking what I had been told about its changes: a casino, hordes of people, motels, snack bars.

But when we walked from our hotel to the quai de Barthélémy, it was almost exactly as I remembered it: fishing boats dancing on the blue water and rubbing their sterns against the stone wharf, ready to sell their catch; flowers spilling from balconies over a café terrace. . . . It is still here, I said to myself. Nothing has really changed. War and even Time have not touched it.

There were the furled sails, the hawsers, the morning's shimmering catch ready to be sold, and the little terrace waiting for us to sit on it. Five lemonades and one pastis. . . .

"Look," I said to my troupe. "This is where the rope is tied around the hawser to hold the boats safe to the quay." And I sat on one, and it was made of papier-mâché and plainly phony, and in a cloud of embarrassment, of mild mockery, I was led around the bend of the port to a big empty shaded terrace on the quai des Baux, across the street from a café I remembered, or thought I did. There were sliced shadows across the tabletops, like the beach scenes from *La Dolce Vita*, and I felt lost in the flight of the years.

Somebody brought us drinks, after we had crossed the street to ask for them. We were told that *Fanny* was being shot, with Chevalier, Boyer, others. The plastic flowers, the old boats, the indestructible fish, the cardboard hawsers—they all fell into their own focus, and I felt less foolish, less fooled.

And then you, my dear Maurice, walked lightly under the thin bamboo roof and sat down at the other end of the empty open room from us, with two little girls. I knew you at once, and my heart jumped, then paused, and then lay still and waiting, exactly as it had in the dark Pasadena movie and the bright Hollywood corridor. You were as young, as superbly nonchalant and controlled, as subtly wise as ever.

Once more I pretended not to be there.

I have always been sorry for this final timidity. I am sure that there could have been a bright moment for the children and for me too, because you would have been courteous, as always, and we might have given you some fleeting amusement: five new people to smile blissfully at you, and at me their shy duenna. You would have recognized me, in spite of my obvious middle age, as another child crying out, "Look! There's Maurice!" You would once more have sniffed "the perfume of being human."

My two girls were sizing up the ones you were with, possibly a director's children, and there was that strangely wary atmosphere between our tables which, in older female lives, is kept less overt. One of my daughters finally murmured to me, "They are American!" She sounded a little toplofty, and I asked mildly, "Like us?" She laughed and then said, "But the man is look-ing at you as if he knew you." I felt flustered, but answered, probably with an extra swig from my glass for courage, "He doesn't. But it is Maurice Chevalier!"

My girl gasped, in admiration and envy—of you, of me because you looked across at me so benignly, of life in general. All the children stared as politely as possible over the rims of their glasses.

Then is when I should have given you a genteel but still happy smile and walked across boldly to your table and said something silly, probably begin-ning with "Oh. . . ." Yes, I should have done it. Our companions were all of an age, and it would have been good for mine to meet somebody from the country they had not seen for a long time. And I myself was old enough to do more than simply sit there in the stripes of sun and shade, my heart thumping, my hard-earned poise cowed by my admiration and my love for you!

I am reasonably sure that you were quite unaware of anything about that peaceful empty terrace that you could relax in a quiet place away from the cameras for a while, with two nice kids and a few more across the shady way, sitting with their mother or nanny or somebody. If they stared a little, that was part of your way of life. But I, on the other hand, felt a wave, a current of real charisma-charm-empathy flow from you toward us, the kind that almost commanded me to walk toward you, smiling gently as you were smiling, warm as you were warm. Stupidly I let it turn into a Lost Moment.

This has always been a small sorrow for me, that I was so timid, so slow—afraid of spoiling your calm pause from the job, of embarrassing the children, of being politely removed by a bodyguard.

But now I have a chance to work for you, no matter how indirectly. Your publisher in America has suggested that, because of my real love for that young charmer well into his eighties when he wrote the book, I might like to write some sort of preface to your text. I could have shouted with joy. I need not wait for Heaven to be rewarded for my four full decades of devotion!

This is all right, culturally if not as a matter of strict decorum: I speak for countless women in my country—and for men too, who ask me with spontaneous candor to give you their love with my own. That is part of your ageless magic, that everyone who has ever met you, in a theater or movie or newspapers, seems to feel as pleasurably enamored of you as I do. You have written your own love song to Paris, and here is ours to you, in my words but for all of us.

Sincerely,

[signature]

Thine forever,

[signature] Mary Frances

1978

Soup and Bread

ONE HUNDRED RECIPES
FOR BOWL AND BOARD
by JULIA OLDER AND STEVE SHERMAN

This foreword for a book called Soup and Bread, One Hundred Recipes for Bowl and Board *I did partly because I admired both Julia Older and Steve Sherman, but mostly because of my really great respect for Stephen Greene, who printed it in Vermont in 1978.*

That year the Stephen Greene Press sent me the proofs of Soup and Bread, *and I agreed to do a little preface for it, partly because I was writing more easily than in my first rather stiff and formal thing for my godchild Sylvia Thompson, and partly because I also liked the people who wrote it. They were adventurers. Once they walked and rode on bikes and backpacked on the old Appalachian Trail and produced a memorable book about that. And this one about soup and bread was interesting, and of course well written and rich with good recipes. I don't know if many people ever read it or bought it, but I loved doing the preface. I don't think I got paid anything for it, but I would not have wanted to take money, mostly because I admired Stephen Greene and all others so much.*

I think by then I'd met his daughter Stephanie, whom I still know, too vaguely because she's back in Vermont and I'm out here in California. She was a student in Berkeley at the university, and I remember she told me about how she'd been pestered to join the Unification Church. (We'd known about it in France too . . . nice-looking young people would pop out from behind corners or into cafés trying to sell us their newspapers about The Movement. . . .) Stephanie said her student friends were all smiles, and invited her to go on long wonderful weekends with them, but she knew that they were trying to convert her to the religion of their leader, the Reverend Sun Moon.

Steve Sherman and Julia Older write now and then to me, and I love keeping track of her good poetry and whatever they both are writing. Most of all, though, I think strongly of how brave and fine Stephanie must be. After her father died in a bad plane crash that also killed off most of the cream of American publishers and editors, who were heading for the annual American Book Association meeting on the West Coast, Stephanie stood by the mass grave that held what could be collected of all these famous people, and conducted a very simple ceremony that laid them to rest. I sometimes think of this with wonderment.

A FOREWORD

It is impossible to think of any good meal, no matter how plain or elegant, without soup or bread in it. It is almost as hard to find any recorded menu, ancient or modern, without one or both . . . just as it is to read a book, or walk through a museum, without savoring one or both on the page, the canvas . . . the mind's palate.

Of course bread and soup, being thus intrinsic to our survival, can be deeply personal things to the fortunate among us who are blessed with fearless memory. We read, for instance, about a soup served to an Egyptian princess or a Roman tyrant, or about bread broken long ago in the country called Israel—and then we taste, according to our cultural empathy and our gastronomical curiosity. But what we savor more keenly than these, if we are both lucky and honest, is a dusty soda cracker stolen from the pocket of a fat schoolfriend (shamed delight), or two bowls of a rich vegetable broth drunk lickety-split after a childhood fever (voluptuous satiety).

I have always been fortunate in this trick of recalling past pleasures, especially in times of inner drought and stress. They are food for the spirit. This is one reason why it is satisfying to find an intelligently compiled, sensitive, practical book called, with a simplicity that is reassuring, *Soup and Bread*.

It is evocative, as all good things should be . . . on the page, the plate, the mind. It is well put together, so that a soup, and a good bread to go with it or even to follow it, face each other on the pages. Nobody need agree with how the authors have paired their recipes, for they can be used in any personal jumble. I myself would not like a Sally Lunn with Artichoke Soup; that is, my mental taste buds say that I would not. But I must think more about it . . . try it. . . .

The book evokes enjoyments, sensual memories. There is a good recipe for *Pan Dulce*, for instance, and reading, once more I am in the early market in a Mexican village, buying a warm sweet roll from a woman who walked for hours down the hills with the night's baking in a coarse cloth on her head. The bread was spicy, surprisingly rich for that spare country. I ate it from a piece of oily newspaper on the counter of a little open-front bar, and drank a local beer with it instead of the thick *sopa* suggested in this book, and it was a long time ago, but the taste of coriander and dark sugar and just-baked dough is still fresh.

It seems strange to me by now that when I was a child we were rescued by Sustaining Broths when we had been ill, and that the only real soup I remember eating with my parents was a rare Oyster Stew on the Sunday nights when Grandmother, our gastronomic mentor, was away. Of course, when I was drinking the invalid broths and downing the memorable Oyster Stews of my early days, the question of finding good bread was not yet dreamed of. Bread was good, that's all. The flour was good, and so was the water. If the current cook did not have a light hand with the dough, there was an excellent baker in town. Toast for breakfast, treats after school with strawberry jam, dried crusts for Bread Pudding stiff with raisins: we never *doubted*. We thrived.

Our gamut of baked breads was as limited as were our soups, almost: white, Graham, now and then hot baking powder biscuits or corn bread. The last two were "special" and served only at noon, but the others were ubiquitous. They were *there*, supposedly our right and privilege.

Once a very old woman told me what her even older grandmother had told her about Bread Soup. Across about a hundred and fifty years I heard again of the most comforting thing that could be eaten on this earth, at least in the days when the makings were unpolluted: broken pieces from yester-day's loaf, in a bowl, with a ladleful of boiling water poured over it and, on a feastday, a sprinkle of salt. This, the old, old woman told me through generations of gradually corrupted palates, was the best food in the world to comfort and bring sweet sleep.

Such a recipe is not found in a collection like this one. Indeed, its austerity is almost impossible to evoke with the mind's palate, so far are we from the child of 1830 who could find celestial what we would call prison punishment. Today's bread, today's water, even the iodized fluoridated salt? No.

That is another reason why this book is worth pondering. It nourishes us with simplicity, adjusted to our times, but also with many subtleties that are as amusing as they are plain. Why not put canned apricot juice in Cock-a-leekie Soup? It is logical, if you can read. And why not serve beer with one soup, milk with another, a Zinfandel here and a sparkling wine there? And the suggestion that sweet butter and wild grape jelly would do well with popovers! It is so sensuous that the scalp prickles . . . centuries from a child's dream of bread-and-water. . . .

We can be helped, in this less innocent world, to reach back a little in a book like *Soup and Bread*. Why not make something like Vegetable–Short Rib Soup, and some Wheat Germ Crackers . . . find some good cold milk . . . help a child of this century rise again?

Not a Station But a Place
drawings by JUDITH CLANCY

In 1979, I did the introduction for Judith Clancy's drawings of the Gare de Lyon, and called it, and the whole book, Not a Station But a Place. *Then later it was used as an essay or story in another book of mine. I enjoyed enormously writing it, and I did it to point out the value of the drawings, as well as the value of the place, the station.*

There was some talk that the new Pompidou Museum in Paris wanted to add the book, in French of course, to the permanent exhibit of French railroading stuff. It would have sold very well, not only there but also at the Gare de Lyon, and in both languages. So I asked my friend Madeleine Grattan, of Aix-en-Provence, and now in a New England college, to do a translation.

I thought her result was masterly; she caught my use of the English language very well, in French. (It was better than what I wrote in my own tongue!) Flammarion and two or three other publishers were interested in doing it. But Judith, without telling me, decided to add several collages at the back, and some of her own prose. There would be a "collage" of a matchbox, a photograph of her getting off in the station in Rome, a crumpled Kleenex because she had a cold. The French

editors said, "What's the point of these? They have nothing to do with the book
. . . with Paris." And the whole thing was dropped, to my great regret. I am still
embarrassed about Madeleine Grattan, because she should be paid for the work
she did, even if it was never printed. I hope this project will be revived, because
the drawings are very good.

In 1986 Judith Clancy had a show at the Musée Carnavalet; she is the only
American woman to have been thus sponsored by the French government. Un-
fortunately, it opened at a time when Americans were not supposed to like the
French, since France had forbidden the English prime minister to unleash a pack
of Yankee planes to fly over its territory, during the elections, to a rendezvous
outside of Libya. It was one of those gigantic attempts at diplomacy by clumsy
people, and one of its tiny results was that the Clancy show opened to an almost
empty house. Few Americans came, except for our ambassador. And then there
was supposed to be a garden party, and it rained. Of course, things like the weather
and international good manners changed and later all went well . . .

Whether the French opinion about Clancy's collages in Not a Station But a
Place *will also change I have no idea, but publishers in Paris still sniff about,*
and the drawings are fine in any language. The book is good, and it was both
drawn and written with love and passion, because Judith and I love the station
and the place. And so does our friend Madeleine Grattan.

Paris fairs and expositions, always attempted and sometimes realized on a
grand scale, have been beset, at least in the twentieth century, by strikes, riots,
floods, and other natural and man-made hindrances to such minor goals as
opening on time. In the same way, they have left something strong and beautiful behind them, whether tangible or in men's minds and hearts.

In 1937, for instance, there was the *Exposition Internationale*. Strikes were
an almost stylish necessity of life in those quaintly distant days before all
Hell broke loose, and the fair lagged in summer heat while opulent or simply
eager tourists marked time in the cafés and museums; outlandish buildings
were put up and torn down and picketed and sabotaged. I was there from
Switzerland to meet my parents, who loved great fairs, as do most mid-
westerners reared on St. Louis and Chicago and even San Francisco shiv-
arees and suchlike rows, and my father was excited by the violent scornful

unrest in that year's Parisian air, as he had never been at home by giant me-
chanical toys like roller coasters.

We walked every day in the purlieux of the exposition, to guess when a
pavilion might possibly be opened or bombed. At night we looked at the
lighted revolving statue of bright gold in the U.S.S.R. exhibit, but Father
did not want to visit it, for vaguely political reasons. Once we went on the
Seine in a *bateau-mouche*, and he was thrilled when every window in the
Citroën plant was filled with striking beleaguered workers saluting us with
raised fists. Nothing like that at home!

But from that fair, which never really came to life for us who waited, rose
one bright star, the *Guernica* mural by Picasso. It was there. It was on view.
It was well guarded. It was moving and terrible, and we went perhaps five
times to look slowly at it, close up, far off, not talking. It was a difficult experience for my father, but one he faced with an almost voluptuous acceptance, so that we began to return compulsively to the long room where the
painting unrolled itself. There were piles of rubble and discarded tools on
the unfinished paths outside the building, but inside, people, even those
from Iowa and California, walked silently up and down, finding parts of
themselves in Guernica.

Backwards to 1931, there was a fair called the *Exposition Coloniale*. As
far as I know, some of it opened more or less on schedule, at least in time to
assemble peculiar exotic hints of the imminent collapse of French attempts
to keep their own sun shining around the clock on territorial land-grabs.
What else could it try to demonstrate? Why else would a reputedly thrifty
nation spend hundreds of thousands of francs recreating African villages
and Indo-Chinese temples for visitors to gape at? From now in Time, it all
seems to have some of the luminous gaiety of a terminal cancer patient's
final defiant fling. I lurched about on camels, and watched silent blacks
squatting in front of their phony huts to carve cabalistic masks. Everywhere
there was a heady perfume of leather, of raw silk and wool, of unknown
spicy foods. As in the *Internationale* that came so few years afterwards, the
Coloniale had a dappled green magic, under the summer leaves, and left
behind it more than its rare polished woods and supple cloth.

But both those fairs seemed unreal. They were *there*, in spite of strikes
and riots and general political uncertainty, but where are their physical
traces? Where is the cardboard Angkor Wat, now? The painting of *Guer-*

nica still exists, but where is the long shady building that harbored it? Where is the golden statue that revolved seductively, almost lewdly, above the Soviet pavilion? In the end, where are the dreams and wars that spawned all that pomp?

It was probably different in 1900. The hunger and shame of the Franco-Prussian War had been half-forgotten by a new generation, and the Dreyfus Affair seemed temporarily under wraps. Paris needed and indeed deserved a circus. Architects were appointed, perhaps subconsciously, who could evoke all the rich weightiness of the Third Empire, before the late and current troubles, and they put together some pleasure-domes for their fair that still enchant us: two palaces, the *Grand* and the *Petit*; the bridge across the Seine named for Alexander the Third; best of all, to some at least, the Gare de Lyon.

It happened before my time, and the French accounts are understandably vague about how and when that World's Fair finally ground into action. It seems natural, by now, that the enormous glassy station was formally inaugurated a year late, but it is still there to prove that in 1901, on April 17, the president of the Republic and countless international notables gathered in it to declare that the Gare de Lyon was indeed a reality.

No doubt other very solemn things have happened there in almost a century, like treaty signings and top-level hanky-panky connected with both railroads and people, and municipal banquets, but it is hard to imagine that they did not contain a certain element of enjoyment, in that magical place. Surely the ceremonial toasts tasted better there. . . .

As far as I can know or learn, no other railroad station in the world manages so mysteriously to cloak with compassion the anguish of departure and the dubious ecstasies of return and arrival. Any waiting room in the world is filled with all this, and I have sat in many of them and accepted it, and I know from deliberate acquaintance that the whole human experience is more bearable at the Gare de Lyon in Paris than anywhere else. By now the public rooms on the train level are more plastic-topped, chromium-benched, than in the first days of wood everywhere, with iron and brass fittings. But the porters seem to stay sturdy and aware, and there is a near-obsolete courtesy at the "snack bars," even five minutes before commute time.

For me, it began to come to life in 1937. I was there often, from 1929 on, always one more ant scuttling for a certain track, a cheap train south to Dijon, a luxury train to Lausanne. The station was something to run through. It was a grimy glass tunnel, and I felt glad when we pulled out and headed south.

But in 1937, when I could meet my parents in *La Ville Lumière*, I grew almost shockingly aware of the station. I went there early that twilight, for their boat train from England. On the *quai* that looked far out under the glass roof and along all the gleaming tracks was a café, part of the big noisy bar-brasserie inside. There were little trees in long boxes, to sweeten the air and catch the soot, and the tables were of that gray-white marble that apparently was created by Nature solely for café tabletops. I sat waiting, drinking a brandy and water, realizing suddenly that I was not in a station, but in a Place.

My family arrived, worn after a rough crossing, and it was not for perhaps ten days that I went back. My father was going down to Nice. For the first of countless times I cunningly arranged our getting around Paris so that we would have to *wait* for the train to slide in under the glass roof along the silver track, so that I could be there . . . in the Place.

It was one of the pleasantest times I'd ever known with a man I'd always respected and loved. We were two people, suddenly. We sat behind the boxes filled with gritty treelings, and although it was only late morning we drank slowly at brandy again, with water and casual talk and mostly a quiet awareness of the loveliness of the great station.

It was not noisy. It was not stuffy. People did not look sad or even hurried. Trains whistled and chugged in and out, slid voluptuously toward us and then stopped. Big boards lit up here and there, high above the tracks, telling people where to go, when. A porter came to tell me that it was time for the gentleman to board.

"This is the way to do it! How can a railroad station be so beautiful?" my father asked happily, and I knew that I had marked off another mile in my life.

Then there was a war, and when I went back to Paris in the early fifties, I scuttled through without more than a shy shamed look at the glassed roof that the Occupiers had found too essential to destroy. I did not permit the station's magic to take hold again until about the mid-sixties, when I went alone to Paris, for the first time in my life: no husbands—lovers—parents—children . . . I was on a writing assignment, and I asked to be lodged in the attic of a hotel on the Seine in a room I liked most. My husband and I had planned, before the war, before he died, to rent two little connecting rooms there and make a kind of pied-à-terre, a place where we could leave books and be warmer than in Switzerland. This all turned impossible, and when I went back so much later I felt scared, so that I asked to take one of those familiar rooms. And in the other, to my astonishment, lived a person I admired deeply named Janet Flanner. It was fine. My husband would have liked it.

And so it happened that I reported, that summer, to my friend about my love affair with the Gare de Lyon, and she in turn decided to take her own look, which she admitted had always been a sketchy one in spite of some forty years in Paris, and with due reflection she reported the whole thing to André Malraux, who then controlled the governmental wires that could declare a French relic or monument legitimately "historical," and therefore supposedly immune to further human destruction.

Malraux had a rare and passionate belief in "the redemptive power of beauty," and seemed to know that a minor living art form is far more vital than a major dead one. From what I have been told, he started at once to safeguard the shabby old restaurant in the Gare de Lyon, so that by now it is a twinkling "*Monument Historique*," worthy of all that was opulently cheerful, generously vulgar and delightful, about the Belle Epoque.

Things were different from my lives before, in the mid-sixties. The job demanded that I go between Paris and the south quite often, and I was looked at as freakish because I insisted on taking the Mistral train from the station instead of flying. A waste of time, of energy, I was told by my bosses. But nobody could understand how totally renewing of many strengths it was for me to go there at least two hours before the beautiful train pulled out, to eat a slow breakfast, and then slide southwards through the forests and farms and into Burgundian vineyards and then suddenly, like an explosion, into the Midi below Lyon . . . and on down, through poignantly familiar towns like Avignon to the spot past the Etang de Berre, just before the Quartier de St. Louis in Marseille, where there is a mysterious flash of gold from the tiny needle of Notre Dame de la Garde.

From then on it was less emotional sailing, with cliffs and twisted pines and strange villas, until I got to the familiar little station in Cannes and the resumption of my professional life, but always I felt brave enough for it, after the private meal in Paris.

The main room of the First-Class Restaurant-Buffet at the Gare de Lyon seems to run the whole length of what to us Americans is the second floor. Actually, if one enters by way of the noble staircase from the inside *quai* of the station, there are several rooms of varying importance to the left, closed and reserved for board meetings and other mysterious gatherings. Mostly, pundits and tycoons heading for them use a smaller staircase that goes up under the clock tower, and never set foot in the enormous restaurant. (The Big Ben Bar and the cloakrooms are conveniently to their right as they enter!)

To the rest of us travelers, going up the staircase from the *quai* is much more exciting than the handy little "back stairs," and the huge room sweeps out, dreamlike and yet inviting, and across from us the lace curtains move faintly in the drafts from the great square below.

Down at the far end, to our right, the Train Bleu is properly hushed and somewhat more elegant, if that is possible, than what any traveler can expect in the main room, only tacitly separated from its little offshoot. Service is swift or slow, according to one's logistical needs, and there is a comfortable feeling of bourgeois polish and sparkle everywhere: clean linen and brass, waxed floors, good plain food as well as a few fastuous dishes. Mme Maigret would approve of it. So, I feel sure, would Brillat-Savarin, if it were not some 150 years too late. . . .

It is one of the most amazing public dining rooms I have ever seen, or even imagined. The ceiling is very high and elaborate. The windows are tall, looking on one side upon a goodly part of Paris, and then to the right into and under the endless stretch of gray glass roof over all the tracks that come to a dead stop down below . . . England, Switzerland, Italy, Spain, the Near East, all France to the south. . . .

The walls, between and above the great lace-hung windows, are covered with more than forty huge murals of every possible scenic delight that the Paris-Lyon-Mediterranean trains could offer their travelers at the turn of the century, mostly peopled by plump Edwardian diplomats in top hats, and famous divas and courtesans in filmy garden-frocks or even bathing dresses, all frolicking discreetly against breathtaking landscapes.

By now, the paintings have been cleaned, and their elaborate frames retouched. The lace curtains have been mended and starched and rehung, and the three monumental ceilings with their "crammed and gorgeous" paintings have been pulled back to life in our comparatively clean air, after years of collecting soot from the old steam trains below. And all the elegant *bancs* and chairs, comfortable in dark soft leather, have been refurbished, along with the sumptuous but functional brass racks for luggage and hats, and the tall lampstands along the middle aisle.

Perhaps best, at least for the waiters, is that the endless polished floors underfoot have been strengthened or repaired, so that there is no longer the steady creaking that I first noticed, when I listened there in the sixties.

I am not sure, by now, why I first decided to go to this station two hours before train time. Perhaps I wanted to sit where I had once been with my father. Perhaps I wanted to ready my spirit for the new job in the south. A porter (Oh, a fine man, an angel in a blue soft blouse! I remember him clearly: tall, past middle age, oddly protective of me as was exactly right on that day . . .) told me when I asked to follow him to the café on the inside *quai* that he thought I would be better off upstairs, where he would come for me in ample time before the Mistral left. I felt docile, and followed him under the clock tower and past the end of the big noisy brasserie-café on the ground floor and up some back stairs, into the shrouded silent corridors of the first-class restaurant. I had never been there before.

He pounded on ahead of me with my luggage, and a waiter who knew him came from somewhere past the deserted old Big Ben Bar. My porter went straight down the middle aisle of what seemed like a silent gaudy cathedral to me, and stopped toward the far end, which as I remember was being remodeled for the new Train Bleu section.

"Madame is hungry," he said in a mild way to his friend. "She is taking the Mistral. I'll be back." I felt helpless but undismayed. This was part of important private history, I sensed.

The waiter was surprisingly young to be working in such an awesome monument. He gave me a menu, and I settled myself in the huge sunny temple while he went down to the newsstand where I had planned to sit in all the sooty racket behind a spindly box tree, drinking *café au lait*. When he came up again with two very solemn daily papers, I told him that I would like bread and butter, Parma ham, and a half-bottle of a *brut* champagne that seemed quite expensive to me and that is no longer on the excellent wine list. He looked pleased, and scudded off, with the floor under him making a fine high racket in the emptiness.

In 1967 or whenever that was, I felt dismal about the state of bread in Paris, and had not yet found that it would be almost as bad everywhere, and I decided then that the fresh loaf served at the Gare de Lyon was the best I had tasted since before World War II. (It still is.) The butter was impeccable, not something from a tinfoil wrapping marked with either optimism or blasphemy *Beurre d'Isigny*. The ham was genuine, perhaps tasting of violets on the wishful tongue. The champagne seemed one of the best I had ever drunk.

The waiter saw that I was more interested in where I was than in where the grim newspaper editorials were telling me to be, and he stood tactfully beside the table while I asked him about some of the murals. He knew a lot, in a controlled but fervent way that I had long recognized in devotees. Now and then he flicked at one of my crumbs, to stay professional.

Then the handsome, thoughtful, strong, blue-bloused, honest, punctual porter beckoned to me from the gigantic doorway that opened onto cloak-rooms and the Big Ben Bar and the far, closed doors of a Belle Epoque palace, and I left without sadness, knowing that I would return. I turned back at the end of the corridor, and the waiter lifted the bottle of champagne where I had left one glassful, and bowed and smiled. I felt fine about every-thing, even my job . . . generous, warm, floaty.

The next time that I cannily arranged to be in Paris so that I would have to take the Mistral again, I went somewhat earlier to the station. I forget whether there were only two waiters that morning, or whether it was later on, when I suddenly looked up from my habitual little meal and saw four or five of them drifting around the table. Mostly they were young, but there were some old ones too, and they had decided they knew me, and what they had apparently decided to share with me was horrendous.

The restaurant, they said, was doomed. *"One"*(*"they"* in our lingo) had decided that it was too old to live. The famous lace curtains were in tatters. The paintings were out-of-date, and filthy with some seventy years of soot and general neglect and pollution. The floors buckled under the weight of the men's trays. Yes, a promising young chef, probably a madman like them all, had opened Le Train Bleu. But who but stunned starved travelers would come up to such a drab old wreck as this? "It is a crime of neglect," they said furiously, very quietly, as they stood around my table. "It must not happen. This beautiful thing must not be condemned to death . . ."

I looked at them, so proud, and at the gleaming glass and silver and linen and at my fastuous little meal, and then past all of it to the bedraggled lace, the dim dirty light, the flaking gold leaf above us. I would like to think that I said firmly, "Something will be done." The truth is that I probably whimpered a little as I let the men bustle me down the stairs to the train for the south.

I talked about all this, though, with my Paris neighbor, Janet. I told her about how passionately concerned the waiters were. And it went on from there. And by now the Gare de Lyon is in comparatively fine fettle, no way an aging beauty revived by hormones, but rather a mature female who has survived some unpredictable if foregone setbacks with good health and gracefulness.

Much is going on under the five stories of the mansarded structure of 1900 (". . . a fairly discreet evocation of the Belle Epoque," one government document describes it with equal discretion), and within a few years most of suburban Paris will commute from six deep layers of artful stations being burrowed out, for various environmental reasons. Currently, ridiculous bright orange awnings in a garishly scooped shape have been placed over the seven majestic windows on the "Paris" side of the restaurant floor, but doubtless they will fade, and fall off.

The interior style of this giant station is "pure 1900," whatever that may mean. On the ground floor thousands of people push in and out, buying tickets and meeting uncles and going somewhere, and the café-brasserie is always open and crowded. On the "train" side, the little trees in front of the marble-topped tables were sparse or gone when I last saw them in 1974, and the newsstand did not have its old inky glamour. This could be partly because I too was older and Colette and Simenon had stopped churning out their paperbacks, and partly because travelers do not feel as leisurely as they did when I once sat there with my father. By now there are snack-bar counters inside the busy buffet, and people drink and eat hastily. But a graceful stairway still leads upward, under the glass sky, and instead of one's being alone in the bright huge restaurant, there seem always to be some *people*. They read newspapers or talk quietly at odd hours like my own; the place buzzes gently, like a rococo hive, all carvings and paintings and gilt.

Conceivably gentlemen throng at proper hours around the Big Ben Bar, where "all the cocktails of the Belle Epoque" are said to be served . . . along with the British (and by now international) substitute of whisky-and-water for the sweet pinkish drinks of 1900. (I have never seen a barman there, but then, neither have I seen more than a few travelers in the restaurant at 9:30 in the morning . . .)

Once in the seventies I ate an early lunch rather than a late breakfast in the Grande Salle. It was moderately filled with middle-class people who looked as if they were going somewhere soon, which of course they were. They ate quickly but seriously, in general the *plat du jour*, and read newspapers or peeked at their watches, or talked quietly with Aunt Matilda who was going to see her first grandchild in Montélimar. The waiters glided miles and miles on the gleaming new floors. The incredibly long lace curtains pushed in and out over half-open windows onto the square, but there seemed little city noise. The ceiling with its three enormous murals looked somewhat lower since it had been cleaned, and the walls glowed richly. I walked about, looking at the paintings I liked best, sipping a "Kir au Chablis," and the waiters smiled at me as if they knew we shared a fine secret, which of course they did not know at all. Or did they? (Did I?)

I drank a Grand Cru Chablis, three years in bottle, feeling as extravagant as one of the well-kept women in the glamorous murals high above me, and ate a fine little soufflé of shellfish and mushrooms. Wood strawberries were listed, and their mysterious perfume would have suited the sudden sensuality of the meal, but the waiter shook his head. So I ate dark small raspberries with the rest of the wine, and leaned back to look at the ceiling crammed with color, in carved gilded curlicues, high above the incredible walls covered with their gaudily leering murals, all gold-scarlet-blue, a gigantic jumble of snowy Alps, fishing boats, trains, women, politicians, vineyards . . .

Even in its dingier days since 1901, the Gare de Lyon had stayed alive, I thought, beatifically, and had made tired travelers stretch and smile. It had, one baffled but delighted writer said, "great harmony in spite of its decadent extravagance."

Yes, that was it: a strange massive *harmony*!

I thought of my friend Janet, who had grown angry with herself after she went there to lunch quietly alone, a double wonder for a person of her gregarious volatility. She felt baffled about not using, ever in her long years in Paris, more than the quick dashes through the station and on to the *quais* for trains going south to Lyon and then east and west and on further. She groaned, and scolded helplessly at human blindness.

Often people try to keep secret the charm of a tiny restaurant one thousand light-years from nowhere around the corner, in case there will not be a free table the next time they are hungry for its inimitable broth or brew. But who can hide the secret of a colossus like the Gare de Lyon, where thousands of people rush or amble through it every day, according to the trains they must catch or leave or even think about?

Inside, under the misty glass, in the music of wheels and horns and whistled strange signals, there are signs guiding passengers to the toilets, the newsstand, the café, the buffet, the upstairs restaurant, the Train Bleu. There is no attempt to hide any of this vital and perhaps aesthetic information.

It comes down, I suppose, to a question of where one really chooses to be, and for how long. This is of course true of all such traffic hubs as railway stations, but nowhere is there one with a second floor like that of the Gare de Lyon, so peculiarly lacy and golden. It has, in an enormous way, something of the seduction of a full-blown but respectable lady, post-Renoir but pre-Picasso, waiting quietly in full sunlight for a pleasant chat with an old lover . . .

Something of all this I told to another friend, Judith Clancy, when she said that, like me some years before, she would be alone in Paris for the first time in her lives there. And of course the waiters, old and young, loved her, and she (unlike me, although almost equally shy) made her way straight to the director himself. Doors opened, doors that I had never dreamed of.

At first she was told firmly that she would have to pay for bread and "something else" if she wished to occupy a table for sketching, so as to look respectable, and she agreed happily and proved for several long sessions of eating and drinking and drawing that the creative process is grateful for decent physical support. She coasted on "the best bread in Paris" and carafe-Beaujolais . . . The waiters and the director too came quickly to consider her their Resident Artist, and I could wish to be a small fly watching, perched on one of the murals, except that by now I can see what she saw for me, in her pictures.

They make me long to return. I would be heading for Marseille, and would feel spiritually obliged to ask for a small bottle of champagne and some Parma ham and a roll and butter. One floor down, trains would be sliding in and out under the great glass sky. Far underneath, tracks would still be readying for the new subterranean station. Soon an elegant boat train or a "wagon-lit" would pull in, and people would totter up to the Train Bleu and come to life again like Japanese water-flowers. From outside the gently moving curtains, long and tall as birch trees over the great windows, Paris would breathe into me and revive me . . . as my friend's drawings can do instead.

And who knows when the next fair will be, in Paris? Perhaps it has already taken a different shape in the human soul, like Pompidou's Beaubourg or even the airport named for an earlier leader, Charles de Gaulle. Architecturally these two monuments are more than a century away from the railway station built in 1900 in belated obeisance to Louis Philippe. It is a remnant, massive but strangely lightsome, of the ponderous memories of the Third Empire. Perhaps it was offered to the nation in place of another Roman show. So, in a way, are new airports and cultural centers. They all may serve to calm our fears about the future, to amuse us today. Circuses are fun, and sometimes they last longer than anyone thought they would.

1980

Japanese Cooking
A SIMPLE ART
by SHIZUO TSUJI

In 1978 my sister Norah and I went to Japan for about eighteen days. This was because many years before I had promised Shizuo Tsuji that if he wanted me to do a preface someday for his unwritten masterpiece, whatever it might be, of course I would. And late one autumn night he telephoned from Tokyo and said that the book was done and that I must get there as soon as possible. That had been a traveling year for me and I was so taken aback by his abrupt invitation that I said I no longer wished to travel alone, and very characteristically he said, "Well, then, bring Norah!" To my somewhat dismayed surprise Norah said, "Why not?" And off we went.

Of course, we were treated like duchesses, only a rung or two below the Imperial family on the caste-ladder, and I'm sure that I was paid a certain sum as well, although all I can remember is that Tsuji was impassively cross at me for declaring it. He said, "I'll simply hand it to you under the table. Then you won't have to pay Uncle Sam nor will you have to hand that silly 10 percent over to your agent . . ." And he still does not know why I could not agree to his strange un-Western reasoning.

The introduction to Japanese Cooking *was much harder to do than I ex-*

pected, mostly because I was the wrong person to tackle it. I have a rather light way of writing, quite opposed to the pedantic and scholastic tone that was expected of me. Of course, I couldn't say a lot of things the way I wanted to. Almost every word in my whole rather lengthy introduction was weighed and criticized and then weighed again. For instance, at one point I said that a certain percentage of the so-called beef in Japan is really whale or porpoise meat. That was not only weighed and criticized, but thoroughly questioned. One simply doesn't say things like that in Japan. I became increasingly evasive, as I recall, which is basically unnatural to me.

The book was finally published, however (Kodansha International did it in Tokyo, and then it was sent by very slow boat to New York to make it cheaper than any comparable production could have been in America), and working on it taught me a great deal about several other people besides myself. I made other very good friends besides Tsuji-san and his family, whom I'd known for at least twenty-five years: Mary Sutherland, one of the Kodansha editors then, and now even more important in this country; Hata-san, assistant and personal shadow and friend of Tsuji; several wonderful cooks at Tsuji's school in Osaka and at restaurants varying from the Kicho hierarchy to lowly noodle-shops . . . And I'm glad indeed that I had to cope with standards that will always be utterly different from the ones I believed until then were the only ones . . .

I contributed two things to Tsuji's excellent book. At my suggestion, it was called Japanese Cooking: A Simple Art, *instead of something very obtuse and "Oriental." And I sat firmly on the national predilection for camera work, and convinced the editors in Tokyo that line drawings would be much more lasting than photographs. I remember backing myself up in this argument by almost forcibly making Tsuji-san and his henchmen look at a copy of Julia Child's masterpiece about French cooking, in which fine line-drawings were made from photographs of Julia's own hands doing all kinds of wonderful things. The pictures were taken first by Paul Child, the equal of any great Japanese photographer, and then a fine graphic artist took over . . . and I'm very thankful that the same thing happened to Tsuji's beautiful book. (A few photographs creep in, since this is indeed a Japanese work, but they are almost extraneous to the excellent text and the exquisite pictures of "the methods.")*

To sum up what I spent so many really anguished hours doing for my old friend Tsuji-san and one of his many near-classics, I'm proud of the results. And secretly I know that I learned a great deal more than I was expected to, all of which may someday stand me in good stead!

INTRODUCTION

It is strange, and perhaps inexplicable, that a person like me was asked by a person like Shizuo Tsuji to write a preface to his book.

Shizuo was a wunderkind when I met him more than twenty years ago, and by now he is something of an éminence grise in the art of teaching young Japanese cooks to understand what their own food is based on, and where it comes from, and why it can be bountiful or scarce. His school in Osaka is called the Ecole Technique Hôtelière Tsuji, or in another Western language, the Tsuji Professional Culinary Institute. It is impressive, with more than twenty-five hundred students. Their basic education is in their own national cooking, both past and present as well as regional. Once they have passed rigorous tests, about 60 percent of them go on in their native field, hoping to make their mark in Japan's great restaurants, or to inherit their families' country inns, or even to enter the enormous wholesale food industry as buyers or purveyors. Another 25 percent of the postgraduates stay on at the Institute to learn Chinese techniques. The rest, perhaps the most ambitious, study French haute cuisine, taught by the famous chefs Shizuo Tsuji entices to Osaka from Roanne, Collonges, Paris.

And that is the school I went to, for two peculiar and dreamlike weeks in October of 1978, with my sister Norah Barr. I wanted to see for myself what was happening in a chancy modern field of East-West eating.

Aside from our watching some forty-five private demonstrations at the two Tsuji buildings in Osaka (there will soon be another one in Tokyo), and coping with about thirty gastronomical onslaughts, no matter how gently subtle, in restaurants and inns and street-shops, we tasted seed pods and ginkgo nuts, and native fruits like "twentieth-century" pears, as juicy as a ripe melon and as crisp as a frosty apple . . . seaweeds, dried or fresh, poached or swished through broths . . . plum jam, sour as Hell's wrath, in a tiny bowl with two quarter-inch cubes of fried liver from a sea bass . . . the ovaries of a sea slug, buried in froth skimmed from boiling crushed soybean . . . slender cucumbers, faintly sour from their vat of fermenting rice bran . . . ices made from fruit pulps, beaten without sugar and pressed back into their hollowed skins . . .

I was *curious*, and I still am.

Until a few weeks before Norah and I flew to Japan, I had accepted Tsuji's compliments about my way of writing as part of his Oriental respect for older people, mixed with his natural pattern of flattery as a part of good manners. But when he asked me to come to Osaka as a professional, I suddenly realized that he was in earnest about my writing something for him, instead of merely being friendly and courteous.

Norah, who had met Shizuo and who knew of our long pleasant relationship, believes that it is based on a strong mother-son feeling he has for me, something he feels even more strongly for Mme Fernand Point, of Les Pyramides, and most strongly of all for Samuel Chamberlain, who was his "spiritual father," and who is now the constant image of his devotion. If this is true, it is a great compliment to me!

Whatever the reasons, Shizuo did ask me to write some kind of introduction to the two hundred recipes he has chosen, to prove to readers of the Western world that traditional Japanese cookery can and should be a useful part of our own way of eating. At times I am not completely sure that he is right. The preparation and serving of fine as well as routine Japanese food is more obviously mixed, than is ours, with other things than hunger.

At its best, it is inextricably meshed with aesthetics, with religion, with tradition and history. It is evocative of seasonal changes, or of one's childhood, or of a storm at sea: one thin slice of molded fish puree shaped like a maple leaf and delicately colored orange and scarlet, to celebrate autumn; a tiny hut made of carved ice, with a little fish inside made of chestnut paste and a chestnut made of fish paste, to remind an honored guest that he was born on a far-north island; an artfully stuffed lobster riding an angry sea of curled waves of white radish cut paper-thin, with occasional small shells of carved shrimp-meat tossing helplessly in the troughs . . .

All this delicate pageantry is based on things that we Westerners are either unaware of or that we accept for vaguely sentimental reasons. Some of us still eat fish on cue, or matzo, because both priests and parents have taught us to, without much thought about anything but how good they will taste. The past is not as important as the present, nor is religious symbolism open in our thoughts. As children raised in lands of plenty, we do not learn to count on a curl of carrot and one fried ginkgo nut to divert us from the fact that the rest of the food on the plate consists of an austere mound of rice and two pinches of herb paste. We have never been taught to make little look like much, make much out of little, in a mystical combination of ascetic and aesthetic as well as animal satisfaction.

Not only are our ideas of what is delicate and rare different from those of the Japanese, but so is our conditioning. We North Americans, for instance, must combine many ethnical influences in our methods of cooking and eating, because we are all the offspring of other cultures. Our physical habits are different, so that we chew and swallow and sip and raise food to our mouths differently, with different tools.

There are many things about eating in Japan that we either accept instinctively or never learn or care to imitate. It is socially correct there, for instance, to make a loud sucking sound when one eats noodles (or drinks tea, on some social levels). This is basically sensible, since the cool air that goes into one's mouth with the food makes it possible to eat it steaming hot. But such noisy slurping is foreign to our own etiquette.

In much the same way, many Westerners, especially those of us with Anglo-Saxon backgrounds, have been taught not to pick our teeth, at table or indeed anywhere in public. In Japan, though, toothpicks are used almost ceremoniously by gentlemen at fine banquets or in public eating places, with one hand held like a curved fan before the mouth, while the other digs about. Small flat boxes, often very beautiful, hold the picks, which are wrapped in silky paper in fine restaurants.

Another difference, and one that Westerners accept more easily, is the Japanese way of eating, with chopsticks, the solid bits of food from a soup bowl, and then drinking the liquid from it. Like the other habits, this one is practical and simple—as is the custom of holding the bowl near one's chin, or using it as a catchall when transferring food to one's mouth after dipping it in the little bowls of sauces that are part of many meals.

Few people are completely austere by nature, and the Japanese enjoy the way food feels in their mouths and bellies as much as we do. They are basically more aware, possibly, of the functional beauty of a bowl or plate than we are. This does not mean, of course, that when a porter or streetcar conductor stops for a ten-minute lunch at a noodle-shop, he contemplates the pattern of the container, the significant tangle of the *udon* in their clear broth, the cloud-form of steam that rises, the symbolism of all this as a message both from Heaven and to it! He sucks the hot soup in as fast as he can, and pushes the thick noodles into his mouth with his chopsticks, from the bowl held close to it, and then he dashes back to work, untroubled by either aesthetics or an empty stomach.

Celebrations and festivals, though, are times for thoughtful attention, and fortunately there are many of them in Japan. It is then that tradition takes over, as far as modern life will let it, and perhaps an extravagantly lively sea bream will be bought instead of a can of mackerel, and the housewife will shave a cupful of the best dried bonito and use a slice of special seaweed to make a real *dashi*, instead of using a few spoonfuls of synthetic soup-powder dissolved in boiling water.

Mostly, however, festive families will join millions of other people on the city streets and in the parks, and will treat themselves to an extra bottle of sticky soft-drink and perhaps, in honor of Grandmother Itako or the first plum blossoms or the waning August moon, they will buy picnic boxes elegant with chicken, to lay out on a bench, instead of slurping their usual bowl of soup at a street-stand. It is doubtful that many will give a thought to the classical cookery of their country, formalized and artful, which few but the super-rich now taste.

And this is why some scientists and artists and intellectuals are worrying about the present and future of their national food, the Japanese *ryōri*. They hold seminars and debates about the fast-changing tastes in their country. They write books, like the six-volume *Nippon no Ryōri*, edited by Dr. Tadao Umesao, in hopes of showing housewives and even restaurant cooks that convenience foods and microwave ovens and deep-freeze boxes can produce nourishment that need not be robbed of all its traditional taste and interest. Unless such a last-ditch effort works, most of the experts say, Japanese *ryōri*, as it has been known for the past two hundred years, is done for.

This concern for cultural standards is the reason for a book like Shizuo Tsuji's of course. Indirectly, it is probably my own reason for writing a preface to it: I want all of us, East or West, to fight against mediocrity and its gradually lower standards of eating, just as passionately as do my friend Tsuji and his learned peers in both academe and the kitchen.

Shizuo does not expect a hundred million Japanese to crave fourteen courses of airy-fairy fantasy every night for dinner, any more than I expect every compatriot here at home to eat a daily sirloin steak with all the fixin's. We both wish, though, that the staples of our diets could stay honest. In

Japan, *udon* noodles in broth can be delicious. In Italy and France and here, pasta can be fine—and so can hamburgers! The problem is to keep them *good*. The great international companies that will have increasing influence on our eating habits do not seem to care much, if at all, about helping our taste buds stay keen and alive, since if no really excellent food is procurable, they know that we will perforce buy an inferior substitute . . . and second-rate stuff is cheaper and apparently easier to market, anyway.

In Japan, there are not-bad dehydrated foods like soup powders and one-dish meals of wonton-in-broth, which even farm children eat instead of what their parents were raised on. But few manufacturers will bother to produce a commendable packaged staple like plain noodle soup. In somewhat the same way, here in North America anyway, decent bread is very hard to find, unless it is home-baked, because cheaper bread, almost zero in nutrition, is easier to produce and distribute. Everywhere, shoddy stuff is gradually becoming the only procurable substitute for honest goods.

One formal definition of "shoddy" is "transparently imitative." Across the United States, so-called Japanese restaurants serve smelly copies of grease-soaked tempura, and from the Ginza in Tokyo, Big Macs and Kentucky Fried Chicken, fumy with additives and exhausted fats, spread out over a country where for hundreds of years small neighborhood food-shops have provided their own hot bowls and cold snacks, or their local versions of pickles and sweets. Often they have grown famous, as one generation after another has carried on the family recipes, so that canny travelers will stop in a certain village long enough to eat two bowls of a special shrimp soup, or take home some rolls of a fruit-paste that has been exactly the same, past remembering.

Yet the Japanese have long been accustomed to "on the run" eating, and franchised soup-bars and pasta-parlors are now a thriving phenomenon. An American critic who has dismissed fast-food hamburger chains as "the quintessence of shoddiness in our times" warns us, just as Tsuji-san and his peers repeat on television and in university halls, that "by the time shoddiness becomes sufficiently visible . . . its roots have penetrated deeply." And when does "shoddy" become "junk"?

We all ask this. Not enough of us are frightened. But books like this one are written—stubbornly, proudly—by people like Shizuo Tsuji who cannot tolerate letting their national taste falter and die.

Students of the influence of gastronomy on this national taste, and therefore on politics and such seemingly distant subjects, from Brillat-Savarin in France of the early nineteenth century to Umesao in present-day Japan, believe that what and how a man eats in his first few years will shape his natural appetite for the rest of his life. It will not matter if he begins as a potter's son and ends as an affluent banker. If he ate pure fresh food when he was a child, he will seek it out when he is old and weary, it is said. Dr. Umesao cites his own case: raised in Kyoto, where the flavors of every dish are believed, at least by the natives, to be subtler than anywhere else in Japan, he now stays near enough to his hometown to return there every weekend, to buy fish that is fresh enough to satisfy his childhood recollections. In any other city, he says scornfully, the fish in markets is inedible. His palate, he adds, was shaped irrevocably when he was a child.

This theory, which I mostly agree with, has taken a double blow for me because of Shizuo's invitation to come to Osaka. Not only does my palate refresh itself daily with foods almost as simple as the first ones I knew, but I feel that it has stayed young because of my natural curiosity about the best dishes that other countries have offered me. And now, after two weeks in Japan, I must admit with real astonishment that if I could eat as I did there under my friend's subtle guidance, I would gladly turn my back on Western food and live on Japanese *ryōri* for the rest of my life.

Such a pattern would be difficult for me to follow. There, few people without princely revenues and highly evolved palates are served the dishes Norah and I ate. I could never afford to buy them, even as an occasional luxury. For the same reason, neither could I go to the rare restaurants in Japan where such intrinsically *pure* food is still prepared, even if for political or professional or social reasons my reservation might be accepted.

Wealth is so much a part of protocol in Japan that one must know this Personage in Tokyo, that Eminence in Osaka, in order to make a reservation at a certain restaurant in Kobe for precisely 8:10 P.M. six months hence. This is out of my sphere of survival, except for the one such adventure in my life. I know, though, that the food I ate during those amazing days in 1978 has changed my whole palate, or, perhaps the gastronomers would say, it has simply strengthened the taste I acquired as a child? . . .

This is not to say that I could not and would not live well in Japan, just as I manage to do here in the States. I would eat seasonal fruits and vegetables in either place, and honest fresh-caught fish when available, and would surely find a source there for noodle-dough now and then . . .

For the first twenty years of my life I ate healthily of simple good American food. I grew up in Southern California, but our kitchen was generally ruled by midwestern habits, overlaid by Ireland, Pennsylvania, and upper New York State through my grandparents and their forebears. That is to say, we had fresh bread and milk, "produce" from our own or neighboring gardens, and local meat and poultry with their accompanying butter and eggs and suchlike. Everything was taken as a matter of course, with small fuss except on holidays, when for dessert we ate Lady Baltimore cake and ice cream instead of rice pudding.

The next several decades of my life were spent partly in France and French Switzerland, with occasional stays in Cornwall and even Sweden, to accentuate the positive influence of my beginnings. I grew to know, sometimes actively, the ardors and ordeals of cooking in several European and American kitchens, and I went to as many high-style restaurants and hotels as opportunity offered, and read and talked and thought about the art of eating.

The result was that I agreed with my teachers that classical French and Chinese cuisines were the basic arbiters of an educated palate. I knew without any false modesty that my own would never be as well trained as I would like, but I felt no qualms about remaining a willing novice. And always I felt grateful for the simplicity and honesty of my first education in eating. Oddly enough, now that I have found what Japanese *ryōri* can be at its best—that is to say, the perfect food for me—I am not frustrated or sad. Perhaps that is because it is, to be blunt and brutal, almost unattainable. I know that never again can I eat as subtly and exquisitely, in effect, as honestly, as I did for two weeks in my life. That is a fait accompli, a historical fact never to be repeated.

One immediate result of this intense experience is that when I cook for myself now, I am increasingly simple in both the sources of food and its preparation, and that when I must eat in other houses or restaurants, I find the dishes heavy and overflavored, and the supplies not fresh enough. When I first came home from Osaka, it was difficult to use butter, impossible for several weeks to drink milk, unnecessary to pick up a salt shaker or a pepper mill.

Norah and I did not eat only as the industrial princes eat, in Japan. Shizuo sent us for lunches to the *best* noodle-shop in Osaka, the *best* tempura place in Kobe. But his humblest-seeming restaurants, which often seated only five or seven people at a time, were of such high quality that they sold all their scraps, all their used frying-oils and suchlike, to lesser places. Their cooks, who worked across a snow-white cedar counter from us, were the most skilled in the country. Fish leaped from glass tanks to the cleavers and the pans and then into our mouths, in a ballet of accumulated motions and flavors.

After I returned to San Francisco, I went to a stylish new "Yaki Tori Bar," as it was called. Deft young chefs worked in traditional style behind the long dark counter we sat at, and the walls looked mysterious with dim shapes of pottery jugs and bottles, and there was a subtle smell of overused hot oil. The cooks laid little sticks of whatever we had asked for, two at a time, in front of us . . . bits of chicken, bits of fish, even ginkgo nuts, dipped into the suspicious fat and then grilled. Tea was served, or beer. The cups and dishes were very thick and brown, like the place and its pervasive smell, and its ultimate phoniness.

Westerners looked a little shy there, perhaps to watch everything being done so baldly in front of them. There were one or two Oriental couples, possibly Korean. The diners most at ease were an elderly Caucasian and his wife, plainly Old Hands, who used their chopsticks with skill, and seemed to be happy together in a vaguely familiar setting.

It was depressing. I wondered miserably why refrigeration had spoiled so much while it kept things from spoiling . . . why the bits of fish (albacore, it was called on the brown thick menu card) were flabby and sweetish, pulled on their little sticks from a series of iceboxes under the counter . . . why the cubes of chicken (really turkey) were half-frozen even after their oil bath and the ritual of sizzling over the grill . . .

I knew, like a gong sounding far back in my head, what Japanese friends who worked with Norah and me in Osaka had meant when they cursed Tsuji-san for making it difficult for them ever to enjoy wholeheartedly the business meals they must return to in Tokyo. Average-to-good would never really satisfy them again.

I felt lost, full of misgivings about how to explain why I think the Japanese *ryōri*, the basic food that is now in such a state of flux, can be not only acceptable but welcome to our way of life, of eating. Then I thought, as we left the stylish and dubiously "honest" *ryōri-ya* in San Francisco, of how closely the best of Japanese cooking works with and influences the new styles in French and therefore Western food. High priests of *nouvelle cuisine* and *cuisine minceur* are good friends of Tsuji-san, and have worked with him both in Osaka and in their own country. All of them worship at the feet of Escoffier, the first great cook in our Western time to say to his apprentices, "Stay simple! Cook simply!"

The longtime association between the refinements of French and Chinese cooking seems to have shifted to one that is more applicable to our current life-style, so that we now think easily in terms of French and Japanese similarities. We want to make less seem like more. We eat "lightly," compared with classical cooking rules, and in a Japanese rather than a Chinese way we shun many starches, fats, sugar.

We find high style in low calorie-counts exactly right for our repudiation of the Edwardian silhouette (low paunches and high breasts and dangling jowls, and their final reward of apoplexy . . .), and try eagerly to imitate an artful curl of radish and one broiled mushroom elegantly placed on a thin bed of minced spinach as our password to the future. (*Où sont les sauces d'antan?*) Perhaps it started for us with Whistler and the "Japanese" simplicity of his mother's portrait? The fact remains that Zen austerity now intrudes on our old dreams of pastry shaped laboriously into towers of caramel and whipped cream and candied violets . . .

Eastern countries have had more time than Western ones to accustom their people to less rich food than we are used to. Here we load the tables, at Christmas and other celebrations and even for Sunday Noon Dinner, to prove that all's well with the world. In Japan, though, as in many other places on this shrinking planet, there is not space to grow enough food to feed all the people. So one perfect fruit (pear from home, papaya from Hawaii, coconut from Algeria) will be carved and arranged into symbolic patterns that can be religious (intricately Buddhist, less intricately Shinto perhaps), or merely sentimental (falling rain, the first cherry blossoms, a honeymoon in Honolulu). It will answer many hungers, and its design will be savored slowly. And the same dessert, in Paris or Denver, may taste equally delicious because it is low in calories, dietetically safe, a fashionable fantasy, straight from *Bocuse-Guérard et Cie* by way of Kyoto.

Obviously Europeans and Americans are deeply interested in changing their gastronomical patterns. They are sincere, whether for faddish reasons, newly discovered religious or economic convictions, or plain instinct, in wanting to stop eating as much as in the past, and in cutting down their conditioned dependence on fats, dairy products, starches, sugar. Some of them may have flocked like well-heeled lemmings to a fashionable spa in France, and then continued their newfound *bien-être* in the most stylish restaurants of London and New York. Others may have discovered dietary freedom in a hillside commune in California, or a quasi-Buddhist retreat near Barcelona. But all of them practice what they have been "preached," at least for a while, and feel as restored spiritually by their brown rice and herb teas as by more worldly gods and goals.

This free acceptance, no matter how unwitting, of the intrinsic asceticism of Oriental cooking, is suspected by some observers to be a kind of intuitive preparation for the much leaner days to come to all of us who live on a polluted planet. What is now a stylish fad, or an "awakening," depending on both pocketbook and chronology, may become in the future an exotic recollection of the Good Old Days, when carrot curls and cashew nuts were eaten by caprice and not necessity. A latter-day McLuhan might argue that our current preoccupation with culinary simplicity is really an instinctive recognition of our diminishing supplies of food . . . of our need to accept austerity as the rule, after a long time of heedless Western glut.

All this sounds like some sort of celestial plot, a kindly trick of Nature, and perhaps it is. My friend Shizuo Tsuji wants to explain to us (as part of the plot?) his own theory of how and why the Japanese cuisine can be attractive to us. He believes that its combination of subtlety and simplicity has done much to keep Japan a strong nation, especially during the last hundred years of social changes and of revolutions and wars and cultural invasions. Even the Big Mac and Kentucky Fried Chicken cannot displace *udon*, he believes, as long as the noodles stay as honest as the broth they float in.

Tsuji-san is the first to admit to a love of ice cream, and is probably the first authority on traditional Japanese *ryōri* to invest in an expensive Western machine for it, and certainly the first reputable teacher of gastronomy to set his prize pupils to work at devising practical ways to make pure ice cream for their countrymen, without loading it with unhealthy sugar and unaccustomed milk products. He is, like his peers, aware that Japan can adjust to almost any change, and he is determined to keep that change beneficent, rather than let it become one more compromise with mediocrity and shoddiness.

In Japan, red meat has been a status food since perhaps the late nineteenth century. Today it comes from cattle that were originally imported to please foreign palates, or from mammals caught and fast-frozen in far northern waters. It can be superb or routine, like broth made with special seaweed and dried bonito or with a synthetic *dashī*-powder. In other words, one eats according to one's pocketbook—Kobe beef or fish, both prestigious in their own brackets.

This acceptance of imported gastronomical props shows in the three types of popular dishes in Japan, which are not native at all. At least half the population of more than a hundred million people like, eat, thrive on bowl-meals from China (*ramen* in soup), and India (curry-rice), and Italy (spaghetti with tomato sauce). In the same way sugar, which became available to the masses less than two hundred years ago, is now absorbed almost frantically, often as a chemical sweetener and mostly in soft drinks, laced according to their secret formulae with other potentially pernicious additives. Soybeans, which can be called a protein staple of the Japanese, whether eaten as packaged bean curd (*tōfu*) from the supermarket or as a salty fermented paste (*miso*), or as the ubiquitous soy sauce (*shōyu*), used to be bought from China, and now come largely from the Americas.

In other words, cooking is forever a compromise with historical fact and fancy, and Tsuji-san believes that there must be passionate leaders who know how to keep that compromise honest. As a Japanese, he wants his people to remember what has been best, gastronomically, in their history, and try to keep it intrinsic to the inevitable changes of the future.

As an American, a "Westerner," I agree. I want us to keep everything we know of honesty and quality, in eating habits formed during our short history, and shaped by our diverse ethnic heritage, so that we can bow in a basically healthy way to whatever the future may dictate. Inspired French cooks have simplified their art according to Japanese teachings, not too coincidentally, so that now we can eat either "nouvelle" or "minceur" in Pasadena as well as Paris. We can keep our inborn sense of *taste* as a cultural necessity to survival, thanks to the simplicity of flavors and satisfactions we learn daily from teachers who in turn have learned.

Escoffier said, "Cook simply!" The Japanese *ryōri* says, "Let little seem like much, as long as it is fresh and beautiful." The French and their Western cousins look at their medical records as well as their silhouettes, and agree to a new austerity that at its best returns them to a simpler and more honest way of living, and at its worst proves only that shoddiness can never be anything but a transparent imitation of the truth.

An authority on transferring the best of one national cuisine to another (in this case Diana Kennedy, who has studied and written wisely of Mexican foods for American readers and cooks) has said often and firmly that we must never try to *adapt* one cuisine to another, but instead *adjust* the two. As we come to know and use many of the finer things about traditional Japanese *ryōri*, therefore, Westerners can, with few changes in our hereditary conditionings, adjust ourselves to some shifts in pattern and even in behavior without losing our own identity at the table.

Perhaps we can never sit with fascination through fourteen courses of nostalgic nibbles, each with its own place setting and each highly significant in one way or several. Quite probably we can never learn to slurp noodles with correct speed and enjoyment, especially if we were raised in the neo-Victorian tradition. We may never really like chopsticks, which I myself think are fine utensils for picking up small strange objects in the depths of bowls. But just as the Japanese adjusted their palates to sugar as an additive in the nineteenth century, and more lately to "Indian curry rice" and pasta with tomato sauce and even Kentucky Fried Chicken, and hamburgers in buns, and Cokes, so we have adjusted to the imported versions of "tempura" and "sukiyaki" and daring displays of knifework with meats prepared before our dazzled eyes and broiled under our noses.

All these tricks have been adjusted, and skillfully. So why not an occasional long celebration of a birthday in the Japanese manner of a multitude of tiny courses? Why not a full lunch of fresh hot *udon* in good broth, perhaps with some slices of raw mushroom or even a few helpless bay-shrimp turning color at the bottom?

Yes, we can adjust to all this, and we must simplify our cooking just as the Japanese have done, by learning a few more of its complexities, while we still have time.

Vin et Fromage

AN ODYSSEY FOR
WINE AND CHEESE LOVERS
compiled and edited by
MARYLOU SCAVARDA AND KATE SATER

Vin et Fromage: An Odyssey for Wine and Cheese Lovers *was printed in Santa Rosa in 1981, and I wrote a little introduction for it. The reason it was important to me was that it introduced me to several good new people in my life.*

The book was a kind of publicity stunt for the Sonoma County Citizen Advocacy, Inc., and was compiled and edited by Mary Louise Scavarda and Kate Sater. Marylou and Kate wrote and asked if I would help them, then sent me the book, and came down to see me about it. I felt rather impatient: why did I try to help people? We sat shyly by my fire and drank a glass of wine and then I said, "This book is dreadful. It has no form. Whoever is editor simply doesn't know what is going on. You've got to pull it together, so it's not just one more quick thing for a captive audience, the families of the people who compiled it."

Suddenly, I looked at Marylou, who is a tall beautiful dark-eyed Italian girl. Tears were running down her cheeks. Kate sat very quietly, but she was plainly fighting a sense of real outrage. I felt horrified. The editorship had *been awkward and ignorant, but nobody had ever talked to these women so bluntly, and of course*

*they were no more than volunteer agents for a benevolent organization. It was a
very bad moment.*

*Of course, I apologized to them, and we all recovered with well-bred neatness
and dispatch, and I helped them put the book into better shape, and in general
working with them was fine in every way. (Although I remember quibbling a
little about the title of this* Odyssey. *I said, "Why not call it 'Wine and Cheese'?
Why put it into French?" They had no answer.)*

*The introduction was short and fun and easy to do. It gave me a chance to talk
about the real phenomena that such collections usually are. I've looked at a lot of
them in my time, from church guilds and sewing circles and suchlike. I think the
best collection of their titles ever made was done by Eleanor Lowenstein, who
used to own the Corner Bookshop in New York.*

*The book sold very well and went into national production and made a lot of
money for their noble cause, which is as it should be. And it was good for me to
learn that people are much more sensitive than* they *should be, especially when
they volunteer for jobs—such as amateur editors—that actually should be handled by professionals. I'll never forget looking up from my wineglass and watching
those helpless tears roll down the face of one woman who was to be a good friend,
while the other one sat very quietly, waiting to feel less hopeless. It was a painful
and very good lesson . . . I am probably kinder now . . .*

INTRODUCTION

Wine and cheese are ageless companions, like aspirin and aches, or June and
moon, or good people and noble ventures, and this little collection is a proof
of the theory.

The people who have given their time and strength and kitchen magic
to construct it have done so because they feel they are working in a good
cause . . . and few of us can resist this age-old pull, even if it means disclosing
Tanta Rosita's secret spice in her Christmas Eve Mincemeat Tumble.

Of course there is a wealth of such collections as this, mostly composed
by the ladies of the Methodist Circle or the St. Matthias Guild in small towns
all over America. They are a native phenomenon, and erudite cultural studies have been made of them. Often they are ineptly printed and bound, with

well-meant but futile attempts at proper editing. They continue to be fascinating to read, sometimes funny and sometimes revolting enough to raise the hair on one's scruff.

This one, though, is worth owning, quite aside from its historical value. *Vin et Fromage* is a skillful collection of recipes from "home" cooks (mostly) of the Sonoma wine country. I know many of them, and have eaten with them and drunk well of their own wines and other good ones from their friends and neighbors, because one fine thing about vintners is that they are generous appraisers of everyone else who grows grapes, and know the right foods for them.

This is as true in the kitchens of Sonoma Valley as it was and still is in the Napa Valley when I lived in St. Helena, and as it is in wine country all along the West Coast. And it is rewarding to see that it always happens where people keep on trying to help other people. They offer their treasures readily, and put them into a collection like *Vin et Fromage* that is well worth its salt (or basil, or Chardonnay!). They remind us that we live well, out here . . .

1982

The Tea Lover's Treasury
by JAMES NORWOOD PRATT

In the spring of 1982, I wrote an introduction to The Tea Lover's Treasury *by James Norwood Pratt, published by 101 Productions in San Francisco. It was fun to do, except that, because of my "First Reader's Agreement" with the* New Yorker *I had to send it there before I could show it to 101, and unfortunately the magazine took it. I should simply have done another piece, instead of trying to change things around a bit so that it would be less an introduction to a book and more an essay on tea-loving. I thought it would be an easy job, but I'll never try it again!*

This introduction to the Treasury, *though, as printed by 101 Productions, is certainly less correct and less typically the careful, cautious* New Yorker *style of prose in the essay printed by the magazine, which means that it is much more carelessly written. But I like it. It is not bad. I believe that it sold fairly well, although 101 never told me so.*

James Norwood Pratt, who wrote a good book on wines before this one about tea, wooed me outrageously, and even sent me a bunch of American Beauty roses, and we talked often by telephone. He very sincerely encouraged me in bad mo-

*ments, and although I've never heard a word from him since the book came out,
I think we're both living very well without each other. I enjoyed everything except
having to do two different versions, and even that was not time wasted: at least I
learned that a magazine's meat might well be a publisher's poison.*

Introduction

One of the rewards of a long life of trying to use the language with respect
as well as decency is that an occasional invitation is offered to write an introduction to a really good book produced by a younger and more agile
mind. This explanation of my presence in Norwood Pratt's extraordinary
essay on tea is more of an apology than a thank-you, because I have not tasted
even a sip from those cups "that cheer but not inebriate" for more than forty
years. In other words, I have no right to be here at all.

Perhaps this introduction, though, will help to clarify my continuing love
of the brew. If I need an excuse, I turn occasionally to George Saintsbury,
who wrote the small classic called *Notes on a Cellarbook*, although he himself
could not touch wine for the last decades of his life.

Tea makes me drunk, or as I usually think more coldly of it, "drunk as
a skunk." I doubt that it has anything to do with my liver, as was Mr. Saintsbury's reason for total abstinence, but certainly the chemistry of my body
has dictated my sad loss of enjoyment. I found this out, after what seemed
to me at the time (I was then almost thirty!) a long life of true pleasure with
teas, properly brewed.

To start, before my astonishing penance began, I first drank tea at lunch,
when I was between five and eleven. Father came home at noon from his
local daily newspaper, and we all sat down when he did; we ate and talked
and smiled when he did too. And Bertha or whoever was in the kitchen
brought a tall teapot of Dresden china and its matching cups and so on and
put them in front of Mother, at the other end of the quiet but amiable table.
We discussed love, money, and politics after dinner, but never in the middle
of the day, largely because the *News* did not go to press until three, and it
was Father's meal, easy-like.

There was always a pot of cool milk for my little sister Anne and me, because although Bertha served us just as shakily as she did Grandmother and our parents and anyone else there, we alone drank Cambric.

Does this book talk about Cambric Tea? It has undoubtedly been part of all sorts of cosmic finaglings, like the China Trade and other shapings-of-nations, from the nursery on to well-earned serenity and age. A good recipe calls for one part of strong tea in the bottom of a pretty cup or mug, and eight to ten parts of fine fresh warm milk, to be stirred by recipient with perhaps a little sugar or honey and of course politeness.

Cambric Tea, as I drank it at lunchtime when I was little, was a privilege, and therefore lapped up like nectar. It made Anne and me feel almost accepted as people, this cool sop to our nascent self-images. The grown-ups drank it hot and dark, as we knew that someday we would too, and meanwhile our special brew was a fine way to practice.

Grandmother, born in County Tyrone, believed as a good Irishwoman that there were only three kinds of tea fit to drink, none of them store-bought. The first quality was kept, sensibly enough, in China. The second picking was sent directly to Ireland. The third and lowest grade went, of course, to the benighted British. And all the tea used in our house came once a year, in one or two beautiful soldered tin boxes, from Dublin. Then only would we know it to be second to what the Dowager Empress of China was drinking, while the other Old Lady in Buckingham Palace sipped our dregs, as served her right.

Grandmother also believed that tea, when properly made, should be served strong enough to trot a mouse on. I never tasted her noontime tipple, but feel sure that it was as bitter as it was black, beyond much help from milk or even sugar. I knew, though, that it made cheeks pink and tongues looser, as its potency warmed my parents' blood, and I enjoyed their innocent release.

Afternoon Tea was another matter, served to guests who came while Grandmother napped, and I suspect that along with her innate protest at anything English, fifty years on the Iowa prairies had dimmed the Anglican side of her daily needs, if she had ever had one. This was not true of Mother, though, and after Grandmother died when I was about twelve, tea was served every day at four o'clock, instead of at the lunch table. Father was never there, but there was always somebody to share it, in our warm dim living room at the ranch, and I was increasingly on hand to produce it, so that our slavey-of-the-moment could catch a bit of rest before dinner was served promptly at six. Father must be off by seven, to cover the Chamber of Commerce or School Supervisors or Flood Control meetings for the next day's paper. Sometimes the cook and her boyfriend would want to catch a ride uptown to the movies. Dinner, in other words, was hurried and perfunctory if always polite, which may explain some of Mother's sensuous enjoyment of Afternoon Tea, as well as my growing resentment of it.

The truth is that I was a pushover, a patsy, for any kind of slavish house-jobs, so long as I was assured at least weekly that nobody could churn butter on Saturdays as deftly and cleverly and neatly as I, or pick prettier posies, or make a nicer tea.

For several years I battened on this sly usage. By the time I was well into adolescence, though, I began to see where such flattery had landed me, and I went into a long silent emotional simmer. Why was I always the one who had to come in early from playing one-a-cat with the kids on the next ranch, or miss a meeting of the Latin Club, to perform the simple but demanding ritual of making tea for a few old ladies? I knew that I would keep on, because I loved Mother and enjoyed pleasing her, but it shamed me to realize my dangerous hunger for recognition. Of course I kept on with the pesky ceremony, and fawned for more praise by baking dainty little cakes, and slicing bread the right thinness for nasturtium-leaf sandwiches. As I look back on this silently snarling servitude, I think that I even grew the nasturtiums with Afternoon Tea in mind. . . . It was not admirable but it was fun, like scratching an old mosquito bite.

There were several teapots at home. I liked the one we always used for lunch when Grandmother was alive: tall, graceful, with little rosebuds here and there on it, and cups and saucers and cream pitcher and hot-water jug to match. There was a slop-bowl, of course, for the dregs of cups before fresh tea was poured. Then for two or three people, or Mother and me alone, there was the little Georgian silver set. And if duty called loudly enough to invite the members of the St. Matthias Ladies' Guild, there was the ugly big tea set that had been given to one of the Irish uncles when he was Lord Mayor or something. It was handsome and heavy, very Teutonic, not of sterling silver, and usually Mother kept it out of sight.

My favorite was the little Georgian set. It was lovely to touch, and it meant that only a couple of friends might be there by the glowing fireplace, to murmur over their scones and throw an occasional kind compliment toward me. I never joined them, of course, but grew deft at whisking things on and off Mother's low tea table set by her couch.

Cups and their saucers were pure pleasure from the start, and Mother taught me without words that beautiful objects are made to be used, so that even with palsied Bertha at the lunch table, and an occasional wince when a full cup would jig off its saucer before it got down the table to Father, we always used fine Dresden. Or Spode. Or Sevres, from the corner cupboard. Or even Chinese porcelain, designed for the Anglo-Saxon tea trade.

In the glassed corner, both up in Whittier and then down at the ranch after Grandmother died, there was an almost full set of Belleek, sent as a wedding present to Mother. My sister and I stared sometimes at the shells that those cups seemed made of. Who could ever keep the dust from going in and in, like sand, in the wee shells they stood on?

As I remember, the Belleek was used only once, when its Irish donors, rich, titled linen-weavers, stopped for tea in the Far West. The whole idea was a disaster, mostly because the shell-shaped cups, fairylike in their transparent delicacy, kept tipping over on their three little legs made of tinier rosy or pale green shells. The pot, a larger one on three more substantial but still inadequate rosy shells, tipped over. The milk and the sugar spilled. The only thing that stayed upright was the slop-basin, empty because all the tea was here and there on people's knees and laps. And our cook-of-the-moment had tried to follow a recipe for Slim Johns as made in an Irish castle where Mother had once stayed, and they were burned black, inedible.

After the people left, Mother washed the fragile shells herself, and put them back in the glassed cupboard. We never knew whether there was any sand in all the tiny porcelain shells, but we often looked up respectfully at them, and long after our mother had died, Anne sold the set of Belleek to a stylish auctioneer for a startlingly fat sum.

In kitchen cupboards there were always a few clumsy thick cups with deep saucers, which we never used. I still have one of them, for special guests. It was made for Irishmen, Grandmother said, by the same Chinese who sent us their next-to-the-best tea. That was in the days when one was invited to have "a *dish* of tea." The brew was poured into the cup to cool and then it was poured into the deep saucer and drunk from there. I liked the uncouth romance of all this, and of course read sometimes in British novels about a dish o' tea, usually drunk by lower-class characters.

Just lately I read an odd reminder of this, in a novel published in perhaps 1923 by Mrs. Belloc-Lowndes. A Kindly Old Country Doctor comes unexpectedly to the lawn where a lady is resting beside the little tea table that a parlor maid has trundled out to her chair. She is planning or recovering from the addition of cyanide to her enemy's nightly shandygaff. She likes the Kindly Old Country Doctor, and asks him to join her soothing ritual. He says, "I should be glad of some tea. But don't send for another cup. I'll have mine in this basin, for I'm in rather of a hurry."

Basin? Slop-bowl? Shallow saucer? Surely a genteel murderess on a country lawn in the twenties would not have been drinking from a "dish"! Norwood Pratt must be asked about this, as probably the only man in these parts who would know . . .

Myself, I don't have a parlor maid, nor a lawn where a Kindly Old Country Doctor can join me for a basin of tea-without-poison. All this is unknown, where I live, except perhaps for rat stuff. And I do not have a low dim sitting room, much less a sullenly happy young slave of a daughter. I live in a two-room *palazzino*, where people come to eat-drink-talk by a good fire in winter, and in cool breeziness in the hot months, but where serving tea and *then* dinner is too much of a hassle. Where do the tea things go, on my one long kitchen counter where I must cook after the first batch of people? How do I set the round dining table that is between the fireplace and the sink, a few minutes after I have said good-bye to the "tea set" and before I've turned on the oven for dinner? A glass of wine and some roasted nuts . . .

Resentment of my self-invited indenture lessened as I grew up and out, and I made tea almost every afternoon for fellow students in France, because I was a married woman and therefore could invite people to my room when they could not, and also because I had a gas-ring and even running water. And none of us had enough money to go more than once a month or so to Duthu or Michelin, the best tearooms in Dijon, where we would have eaten delicious pastries and ices instead of slabs of the cheapest local gingerbread called *pavé de santé*.

When Mother came to Dijon in about 1930 and saw my prized tea equipment, she immediately bought me four pretty teacups and what she called "a decent pot." I still use it, an ugly Burgundian ceramic thing, but with a good spout. ("It pours well.")

After that, in my thirties and then until death, probably, my bitterness about the ceremony of Afternoon Tea, as seen by the pawn who makes and serves and then unserves it, has grown. When friends will "be along about tea time," often I say, "Or a glass of wine?" But when they mean tea, for cultural or any other of a dozen reasons, good tea is what I give them, and I do it conscientiously and well, and feel about fourteen.

Grandmother taught me, unwittingly, that tea must be hot and fresh, and of fine quality. Mother went on to show me that tea tastes best served from pleasant and elegant utensils. I could never brew tea strong enough to trot a mouse on. Neither would I affect only porcelain, for tea served from a silver or even a pewter pot, if made properly, can be as good as that made in the rarest of earthenware. Water is usually boiled in metal before it is poured over the dried leaves, and then is stirred with a silver spoon, here in the Western world, so why quibble?

My grandmother died before tea bags. I am thankful. My mother never admitted their existence. A friend has described them as boiled mice, and he is right too, but I have some teas in little white bags for people who have never known anything else, and who are adept enough to leave the wee tail hanging over the edge of the cup. I am told that these mice are often dried out and used again . . .

I do not serve the black China tea that Grandmother liked for lunch. Occasionally I serve black Russian tea, but mostly Oriental greens, with beautiful names. I also serve herbal teas made of many leaves and blossoms (everything but alfalfa!), to people who are usually under thirty and prefer mugs to cups and saucers. I even have a silver teapot, although I prefer the good old mustard-and-green monster that Mother bought in Dijon, because it pours so truly.

But I never do more than sniff the stuff, as its first steam rises from its basin. If I did, as I learned some forty years ago, I would probably fall on my face, or go whirling off in a skunk-drunk dance. In other words, tea is my poison.

In about 1942, I spent a night with two friends who were flat broke. I felt poor myself, but did not realize that they actually had no money for toast for breakfast, much less butter or honey to put on it. I was worried for them, but we were young and strong, and we loved each other and still do.

So we sat for about three hours drinking tea. There was nothing like sugar or milk or an old cookie to blanket it. We talked and laughed and came to great conclusions, and I should have remembered how my grand-mother and Father and Mother grew pink-cheeked and chatty after a couple of cups of the lunchtime brew from Dublin. Instead, I finally drove off to meet my mother at Great-Aunt Maggie's and then headed back to Whittier, and almost at once I knew that I should not be behind the wheel.

I was a good driver, and had been since I was eleven and Father taught me . . . pure Hell all the way, since like most loving parents who must cope with preadolescent vacuities he was harsh and mocking. Traffic laws were simple then, and there were no white lines down the middle of roads and no red and green lights. I knew all the rules, including my father's dictum that I should always drive as if everybody else on the road were either drunk or crazy. And that day, full of good company and tea, I knew I was.

Telephone poles were matchsticks, put there to be snapped off at a whim. Dogs trotting across the road were suddenly big trucks. Old ladies turned into moving-vans. Everything was too bright, but very funny and made for my delight. And about half a mile from my long liquid breakfast I turned carefully down a side street and parked, and sat beaming happily through the tannic fog for about an hour, remembering how witty we all had been, how handsome and talented . . .

By the time I got to Great-Aunt Maggie's, Mother was plainly a little put out by my lateness, but I was sober. We drove home in a good mood, and although I never told her why I was tardy, that afternoon we sat pleasurably together by her fire over a good cup of delicate green tea, and she did not see that I was not drinking it, then or ever again.

This deliberate and self-protective abstinence has often filled me with regret. Was I warned so dangerously because of my anger at my own docility for so many years? Did I find myself high-drunk on fury and frustration, or on other chemicals like caffeine? How can I know? And how can a maimed tea-lover like me be writing an introduction to this story of one of the true refinements of our present culture?

Perhaps one answer is that the intoxication that lives in the way our language can be used is headier than any herbal or fermented brew. George Saintsbury knew it, and so do we, the fortunate many. Norwood Pratt's book about tea is written so deftly, in its heady combination of learning and pure love, that its pages will cheer us long after what's in the cup is cold and stale.

Tea grows on bushes, but good books about it do not. This one, though, will cheer us for a long time, and reassure us of the potency of words well used.

1982

Cooking Great Meals Every Day
TECHNIQUES, RECIPES AND VARIATIONS
by RICHARD SAX
in collaboration with DAVID RICKETTS

I don't remember who sent me the typescript of Cooking Great Meals Every Day *by Richard Sax and his collaborator David Ricketts, but I thought it was lively and fun and entertaining, not "important" but good. I said to whomever it was, back at Random House, that I'd really like to do a little preface for it. Apparently they were as astonished as I was at my easy reaction, and they offered me $500, which I took gladly but with more than my usual amount of disbelief in my reasons for doing so.*

I thought that Cooking Great Meals Every Day *had a lot of what is usually called promise, although I knew absolutely nothing about Richard Sax except that he was obviously even younger than he suspected. By now, of course, so short a time later, he is well recognized and has good jobs with good magazines, and the best part of my impulsive reaction is that by now we are friends.*

Apparently this pleasant relationship started when I wrote to Sax and his friend David Ricketts to tell them that a person simply cannot cook or eat a great meal every day. It was almost against their better judgment that they allowed my comment to be printed. . . . Possibly they did so because I am older than they, and they are polite young gentlemen whose manners forbade them, then anyway, to disagree with an old woman. Evidently the publishers found the whole thing amusing . . .

So . . . the two men turned up one day, absolutely exhausted after a wild trip circussing their book for the publishers. (I think "circussing" is an obsolete term for what is called a selling tour, the kind of mad publicity-chase that is considered part of every writer's duty, if he wishes to sell more than a few copies to his family.) Like most innocents, they loved the whole wild scheme, but by the time they got to this obscure stop-off on the West Coast, they could not even remember where they'd been the day before, or whether they were to be in San Francisco the next morning or was it perhaps San Jose . . . or maybe even Los Angeles? . . .

They seemed numbed, temporarily, and sat like two zombies, slumped into opposite corners of my couch. They did not know what they wanted to eat or drink, so I gave them each a glass of cool spring water and waited for it to revive whatever was left of them. When they regained some small bit of consciousness they had almost nothing to say. And before it got dark that day I gave them each a couple of cookies and a glass of milk, and pushed them into their car.

Since then, I've had several good letters from Richard. I often see something by him in good magazines. And I like David too, as Richard reminds him now and then, and I expect another good book from them, whenever.

I still know that nobody can cook a great meal every day, much less eat one . . . and I still like the book.

Preface

The foreword to a book need not agree with its introduction. If I were telling someone beforehand that the writer involved in introducing himself was an idealistic and passionate enthusiast, I might be thought prejudiced, but at least the reader would be warned of my warning. In the same way, my preface might disagree with the writer's book itself, as I happen to do, with complete admiration.

I disagree on two counts. One is that *Cooking Great Meals Every Day* is obviously prejudiced about the pure joys of cooking with both idealism and enthusiasm, and is too generous. It gives so many exciting and logical examples of how to make what Richard Sax wants us to that we risk surfeit in reading it, overwhelmed at times by its suggested possibilities. We need to lie back and digest what has been offered us, before we go forth and try to do likewise.

The other count against this book, which of course can be voiced in a preface but not in the sorcerer's introduction, is that I do not believe a normal human being can eat a "great" meal every day. I believe that everything we put down our gullets should be good, and made of honorable ingredients. It should, in other words, be worthy of its purpose, to nourish us as best possible. But a Great Meal is not an everyday thing. It happens unexpectedly, and the more we understand why it is great and not simply good, the better off we are for the rest of our conscious lives. But it simply cannot and dare not happen on schedule.

It should be like a game, one of the exercises people perform at interviews or in front of cameras or around a campfire, to remember the greatest meal of one's life, or the three or ten. It could be evocative, nostalgic, perhaps even profitable, if all the electronics were in sync, just as it could be plain fun, on a summer night . . .

Yes . . . the first Great Meal in my life! I was about eight, with my father and my little sister, driving in our Model T from the desert foothills of Southern California where a great-uncle had a fruit ranch named Valyermo. Irish Mary, called that to make things clearer between various other females there called Mary, baked a big peach pie for the trip down past Los Angeles to our little town of Whittier, and beside it in the wooden lug-box she put a pint Mason jar of thick cream, with three old chipped soup plates and three spoons and a knife, and we started off, one Sunday afternoon.

The long ride across the desert was not too hot for late August, and Father only had to change two tires before we got to Palmdale. Once down into the winding mountain roads, live-oaks cooled the air, and we stopped at a camp where there were some tables, and ate the whole peach pie, still warm from Irish Mary's oven and then the desert air. We poured cream from the jar onto the pieces Father cut for us, and thick sweet juices ran into delicious puddles. Then we put the empty things back in the box, to wash in Whittier where there was more water, and headed south. Father and I sang "Clementine" and "Sweet Violets" while the little sister slept. We were full of love and warmth and a Great Meal, and no human being can ever hope for more. Even once is a miracle! And once can be enough, of course, but why?

In the case of this book, even if my own feeling is correct that not all meals either can or should be memorable and world-shaking, there is ample proof that no meal ever need be anything but good . . . very good indeed. It is puzzling to me that otherwise sensitive people develop a real docility about the obvious necessity of eating, at least once a day, in order to stay alive. Often they lose their primal enjoyment of flavors and odors and textures to the point of complete unawareness. And if ever they question this progressive numbing-off, they shrug helplessly in the face of mediocrity everywhere. Bit by bit, hour by hour, they say, we are being forced to accept the not-so-good as the best, since there is little that is even good to compare it with. For instance, they say listlessly, tomatoes no longer taste or smell or even look like tomatoes. Deep-freezing and mass production, they say in a familiar dirge, convenience foods and artificial picking/shipping/storing/ripening . . . waily-waily!

And what about housing, to provide for the second of our three basic needs? Where is the warmth and security and privacy that all creatures, even us humans, must have in order to live and die with decency? And as for love, or sex, or whatever it may be called, where is its once jubilant force in our lives, its purity and fulfillment? Ah, waily-o!

And that is why there are books like this one of Richard Sax's, to refute at least a few of the dulled resigned plaints of the citizenry. It is skillful, because he has gone to good teachers and learned well; it is calculated, because he knows instinctively as well as by training what helplessness reigns in our kitchens as well as in our hearts. It is, above all, filled with the kind of ardor that all good priests and healers must feel, to tell us how best to survive.

I honestly do not believe that Mr. Sax, in turn, believes that every meal we eat can be "great." I do know, though, that his methods for showing us to make good things out of ingredients that we take for granted are fine indeed. They are subtle, plain, sometimes lengthy to follow, but oftener as easy as sticking a TV dinner in the oven and making some instant-brew to wash it down our desensitized and sluggish maws. He brings us, to make life better, his own fervent purity of taste, so that we cannot question his firm ignoring of synthetic kitchen-aids, nor his confident assumption that fresh honest decent food is available to all of us, if we will bother to find it.

Rarely does he mention anything that even a crossroads market cannot add to a neighbor's garden or barnyard produce, or to one's own awakening curiosity about making some dish long forgotten, or something undreamed of as yet. There may be one mention of caviar, one use of fresh salmon, in this teasing collection of recipes, but mostly it is about seasonal or all-year foods that are procurable at fair prices almost everywhere in our vast country. When there are no fresh herbs, he uses dried. When there is no good chicken stock to hand, he suggests a commendable tinned kind. And when there is no good meat, he goes without, in a nimble about-face that is skillful and entertaining, as well as fine to savor.

Like any good manual, *Cooking Great Meals* is simple, without long sections on canapés and pickling and so on. If I could make only one change, I would add another little companion to it, the kind that might be bound within or alongside, of all his "basics," his concise instructions about soups, the cooking of meats and fish and eggs . . . They were well worth the price of admission to any show on earth, and what better one than to eat with amusement and satisfaction?

I am preoccupied, as I think about this book and about living well, which I plan to continue to do with increased enjoyment, now that I have stated that not all meals either can or should be *great*. One of the recipes nags most forcefully at me, from all the other tantalizers: the *ribollita*. When shall I try this cousin of Tuscany's bread soup? Who will be here when I serve it forth? What wine will I open for it? And would it be better to wait for a nippy day, perhaps in late October?

I pretend to think of other matters, other more immediate meals. But the recipe nags at me, and I find, almost without wanting to, that I have every ingredient needed for it this very minute, except for the little white beans that make it so creamy and rich. I can get them at the country store and cook them myself, instead of using them from a can as Richard Sax suggests. (His is a practical and good shortcut, but we are partly Italian in Sonoma Valley and can buy every size and color of dried beans from big gunnysacks . . .) So . . . why not tomorrow, or next week? Here are all the vegetables, the herbs, the good olive oil. I am hungry!

I'll need at least five guests, and we can sit in the cooling August twilight . . . perhaps the new people planting a vineyard on the next ranch, and the ex–belly dancer studying to be a CPA and her cabinetmaker husband, and the Buddhist calligrapher? We'll try three wines, and end with a good gutty

Barbera from down the road for the crusty casserole. Why wait until autumn? I must put *Cooking Great Meals Every Day* aside, and make some telephone calls . . .

Brillat-Savarin often said that with a good recipe, miracles might happen. Fresh peach pie in a dusty grove of live oak trees . . . baked *ribollita* on a summer balcony . . . Suddenly a Great Meal again?

Square Meals

A COOKBOOK
by JANE AND MICHAEL STERN

Perhaps I should not say this, because I am very fond of Jane and Michael Stern, but I wish that I had known them in time to write for two books they printed before Square Meals. *It was fun to do, but I really like* Roadfood *and* Goodfood *better. By now, the Sterns are extremely well known, and while they are just as honest and enthusiastic as ever about the real ways of eating here in America (and by real, I mean the honest plain food that we have all known and depended on at one time or another in our lives),* Square Meals *is somehow less vital a comment on our real way of living.*

It is nostalgic. It writes with respect and affection, about things as plain as Celery Seed Coleslaw, Devil's Food Cake, Mom's Chili, Chipped Beef on Toast. I respect it and like it, just as much as I do the Sterns, and my main hope now is that I will have another chance at another good book that they will do. But since they've written about places to get plain food all over the United States in the little quick roadside diners, and then about the same decent solid honest fare that can be found in almost every town in America, and then have written about the square meals we've all had in our time, and the Ladies Lunches, Sunday Dinners, and Suburbia in general, it's hard to imagine what they'll turn up next that I would dare write about. In other words, the Sterns are the ones to tell me if and when I can say anything more for them . . . and one fine thing about my friendship with them is that I know they will, one of these days.

FOREWORD

Dictionaries are always fun, but not always reassuring. This probably depends upon their lexicographers. Our omnibibulous H. L. Mencken, for instance, mentions *square meal* two or three times in his several volumes about the American language, but without really defining it, using it as an interesting proof of our "instinct for the terse, the vivid, and the picturesque," with other scholarly examples like *cloudburst* and *firebug*.

Almost any American knows what a square meal is, whether he teaches computer programming or picks crops. A few days ago a man said to me, "All I really need right now is somewhere to sleep, and three squares a day." And I knew what he meant: warmth, and then food, decent food, something to stick to his ribs and keep him upright and strong.

But he did not mean a bowl of beans, or meat between bread slices, no matter how sustaining either of these things may be. He meant a *square meal*, which perforce means tools and a place to use them, a knife and a spoon, a bowl or plate, and a protected place for the enjoyment of all or almost all he could eat.

Most of us have eaten square meals in strange places. But no matter where we are or how the food looks, we feel without question that it must be eaten while we are sitting down, and it must be ample, to be truly square. It does not matter if we are sitting cross-legged on a flat rock above the Mexican desert, or crouched beside a trout stream in Idaho, or lolled in a diner in Keokuk or Miami or even Beverly Hills. A square SQUARE S*Q*U*A*R*E meal means plenty of good hot or good cold familiar odorous decent FOOD.

Of course this is as true anywhere as it is here in our own country. Sometimes it is harder to find, in far lands. But any man will know, in his own language, what *square meal* means, and will hope to eat one sooner or later. It is human to need one, preferably of familiar foods from a person's past life and yearnings: a platter of noodles, a big plum tart, a slice of baked ham, plenty of everything and the time to eat and then eat more, without pretensions or social prejudices.

We understand what *square meals* are in this country, where most of us have known them from early on and have believed that we could, at least occasionally, continue to enjoy them. The man who told me lately that all he wanted was a roof and three squares a day had just served time in a state prison, where he said he ate pretty well on the whole. But now that he was out again, he wanted his own version of a meal. And I think I know what it would be . . . and so do the Sterns.

On the off chance that my own views of what "three squares" might mean could sound slanted, I have asked a few other native Americans what the term means to them. A ninety-year-old ex-Rosicrucian Buddhist said with enviable repugnance that it must mean a huge hearty feast of meat-potatoes-gravy. Another friend, a plump small-town insurance salesman, said wistfully that it means the chow he got on holidays in Veetnamm: roast turkey, all the dressings, pumpkin pie, first-come-first-served but orderly, in a camouflaged mess-tent in the jungle. Susan, a volunteer lunch-cook in the local grammar school who has been feeding kids since she was kneehigh, thought hard and then said, "It has to be *big*, and it has to be *good* . . . and you have to *want* it."

In other words, the Sterns are right. They have written with love and respect about the square meals of our country, the kind our grandmothers and the ladies of the Church Society and the cookies out in the cattle-country have always managed to serve now and then, to keep us reassured as well as on our feet. Today, many of the things we eat are not exactly as Great-Aunt Jenny made them, but they are still much better than tol'able. Often they come from packages instead of canisters and barrels down cellar or in the summer pantry, but in general the boughten stuff is instinctively rejected if it tastes *too* dishonest, and once accepted by the revered ladies in the kitchens (and by the Sterns!) it is treated with proper care.

Myself, I find this book about square meals, whether we have them three daily or only a few times a year, both funny and useful (as well as of real historical value). Most of us will recognize at least half of the recipes, if we have lived in this country more than a few months, and the nicest thing about this eminently *nice* discussion of how we have adapted our basic frontier-cooking to a gradual sophistication is that it is never mocking or supercilious, never guilty of the discreetly sneering haughtiness I have sometimes felt from people who are insecure about American eating habits.

Here, as in most countries, we eat very simply in rural or ethnic regions. A square meal once or twice a day is something we always hope to provide, and when we can make it for a church supper or a birthday we like to show off and be "fancy." Inevitably "convenience" cans and packages have come into our kitchens, and when they are properly used, they are almost as good as their originals. And of course human laziness is served: for instance, we can still buy unflavored natural gelatin, but many otherwise honest cooks use synthetic "instant" substitutes.

Once I went to a potluck supper for the 4-H club my children belonged to, and seventeen of the twenty women on the Food Committee brought quivering green-and-pink molded "salads" striped with marshmallows and store-bought mayonnaise. Their hardworking rancher husbands circled the three tuna-noodle casseroles like hungry coyotes until the desserts, packaged cake mixes heaped with aerosol Fudge Whippo, were served forth. It was dismal. (I got put on the Food Committee, at the risk of seeming both pushy and protective, and we ladies divided our jobs more evenly and produced some really good meals, hot and savory and *hearty* . . .)

Of course the dictionaries give several definitions of *square*, and a current one meant anything from socially hidebound to plain stodgy, which makes the title of the Sterns's book sound a mite tongue-in-cheek. It is true that a square meal can be both stodgy and hidebound. Basically, though, it will consist of decent bread and butter, plenty of meat/fish/fowl and one or more seasonal vegetables, and then cake or pudding or fruit. This pattern should qualify for what Webster defines as a substantial satisfying meal, I think.

And the food that the Sterns list in their fond and fair and often funny pages is exactly that. It is what we Americans have agreed upon, no matter how grudgingly at times, as a decent facsimile of the plain pioneer food that boosted us through our beginnings. It is familiar, and when we cannot have it we dream of it. We feel OK and unaffected when we confess that we love most of it. It is what we really mean when we half-laugh about Mom-The-Flag-and-Apple-Pie. In other words, a square meal is . . . well . . . who doesn't *need* one, right now or soon?

1984

The BOOK of California Wine
edited by DORIS MUSCATINE,
MAYNARD A. AMERINE,
AND BOB THOMPSON

In 1984 the University of California and Sotheby Publications in London published The Book of California Wine, *after several years of tedious and frustrating work by its three editors, all skilled and noted people.*

The concept of the book was excellent, with an impressive list of contributors writing about every facet of the California wine industry. I was asked to write a preface for it, and of course I was pleased to find myself in such good company. The book is really imposing, and is, as far as I know, a colossal flop in spite of its undoubted historical importance. It is impossibly heavy to hold, and is perforce expensive. Some fine printers condemn it because of its mishmash of types and inks and colors, although it is hard to be scornful about anything designed by the great typographer Ernest Born. (Certainly no one could complain about his beautiful endpapers!)

Mr. Born himself was far from happy, when I talked to him soon after the book appeared. He admitted that he wished more than anything to have a small first run, so that he could improve on the second one!

As it was, I understand that some 30,000 copies of the "first edition" were finally tossed off by the California presses, and that the book was soon reduced drastically in price and that by now it is not selling even for the traditional peanuts. In other words, it's strictly ho hum, *and I feel very sorry about that, because of the long months of suffering it caused many good people.*

As for myself, the short preface I wrote was a pleasant job and one soon done, and from the very beginning I knew that it was completely inappropriate to the rest of the book. It is light and strictly in my own casual style, and rather nostalgic. Often before, I have known instinctively that I was not the right person to add to the scholastic or historical value of a book (I think now especially of Shizuo Tsuji's Japanese Cooking: A Simple Art*), but seldom have I been more aware of how completely out of place I would be than in this impressive tome! However, who cares? I did my best, and the editors accepted it as such, and now, if I needed any solace (and I do not), I know that it is probably the only light touch in an otherwise deadly collection by some of the most famous writers ever drawn together to discuss one vital part of our life: wine.*

A Preface: Wine Is Life

I can no more think of my own life without thinking of wine and wines and where they grew for me and why I drank them when I did and why I picked the grapes and where I opened the oldest procurable bottles, and all that, than I can remember living before I breathed.

In other words, wine *is* life, and my life and wine are inextricable. And the saving grace of all wine's many graces, probably, is that it can never be dull. It is only the people who try to sing about it who may sound flat. But wine is an older thing than we are, and is forgiving of even the most boring explanations of its *élan vital*.

In some ways there is nothing much more encouraging about man's stumbling progress than his growing deftness in making good wine better and then getting it to the mouths and minds of more people. On the other hand, perhaps it has lost some of its mystery and luster in its new availability. The leap from a high priest's sacramental flagon on a marble altar to the plastic container in a motel icebox is shorter than we care to ponder.

Myself, I am glad that people almost everywhere can find potable and honest wines more easily than they used to, even in supermarkets. It was impossible to buy anything alcoholic in Whittier, where we went when I was about four, because it was a town founded by and for the Quaker way of life. My father, Rex, respected this aim, but as a non-Quaker he did not subscribe to it, and some of the best of my young days were spent driving into the beautiful hills and hidden quiet valleys of Southern California with him to buy house-wines. I loved the cold smell of wine cellars as much as I did the fine whiff of ink and fresh paper at the daily *News*.

It never surprised me that the ranchers always seemed glad when we drove up their roads in our open Model T. The women would put tumblers and a long loaf of their last baking, and cheese or a dry sausage, on the kitchen table or under the grape arbor "out back." When the men came with two or three bottles from the old barn or hillside cellar where the casks were stored, they would eat and try the wines and talk. The women and I stayed carefully apart, and I was always given a seedcake or a piece of bread and jam. Finally the jugs Rex had brought along were filled, and sometimes he took older bottles for special days ahead, and we drove away gently so as not to jiggle them too much.

The wines were probably crude and dirty, compared to what we can buy everywhere today. They were unpasteurized, unfiltered, unfined, not made to last long. Although I know that now and then I was given some at the little ranches, well watered to a sickly pink, I cannot remember anything except that I loved the bouncy rides and the fair countryside, and my father for taking me along with him.

My Anglophile mother liked to serve heavy brownish sherries occasionally with desserts, and I was always given a ceremonial sniff or sip, which I still associate with the communion wine I did not taste until after I was twelve, of course, in our small Episcopal church. By then, Prohibition had been in effect for over a year, and we were firmly known in Whittier as the only so-called religious group in town that deliberately flouted the law and served "liquor" from its altar rail. This was, I learned later, because my father, as a respected vestryman, flatly refused to invest in the barrel-washings that were then called sacramental wines, and somehow managed to have a comparatively fine imported sherry sipped from the St. Matthias chalice. It always made our empty stomachs rumble at the Early Service, but at least it was decent stuff, and although Rex himself only went to church on Christmas and Easter mornings, he felt it his duty to protect his elected brethren from what he mildly referred to as Volstead Swill.

Until 1919 and Prohibition, I really enjoyed beer more than I did wine as a day-to-day tipple. Before World War I, I went often with Father to Anaheim, where we filled the back of the Ford with fresh bottles from two or three of the small German breweries there. As I now understand it, this was almost as easy in Southern California as it had been in Albion, Michigan, where my parents had run a smaller newspaper than the *News* and had started a family. There, and then in the little Quaker town, my father put the paper to bed by about three o'clock, six afternoons a week, and walked home to sit on the front porch or by the fire and drink a bottle of beer with Mother. And I got to carry the empty bottle and two glasses to the kitchen and tip back the last few delicious drops of bitter dead brew. (If for no other good reason, this early sampling taught me the mighty difference between real beer and the pale foamy water we now mass-produce in the United States.)

All during Prohibition we kept two decanters on the dining room sideboard, half-filled with fairly good sherry and a mediocre port, mostly used to make an occasional Tipsy Parson when our teetotaller grandmother was out of town. We never drank at the table when she was in residence, out of respect, but that was a time of frequent church gatherings for her, so that almost any birthday or fiesta, sacred or profane, meant a good bottle on the table. We children always had a sip or two in our own glasses but seldom drank them. And Cresta Blanca is the only wine name left in my mind, for a round rich red. The others were unlabeled, from a little vineyard off the Workman Mill road, or Futelli's over near Cucamonga, or Old Man Johnson's back of Corona. They had to be honest to be good, and good meant *drinkable*.

We moved down Painter Avenue and into the country when I was eleven, and as money flowed faster in the decade before the Crash of 1929, the family served dependable bootleg liquor to their friends, and the wines came oftener and tasted more exciting. The two decanters still stayed on the sideboard, and it was understood that if we young ones wanted to drink in our own home, Father would gladly offer what he had to our guests, as long as they knew how to behave. We never accepted this tacit invitation, but as a clear result of it and of our complete lack of any need to find forbidden fruits, my younger sister and I emerged from our Prohibition teens with our livers intact and our palates unscarred by the poison our dates carried in flat silver flasks to all the football games and dances. The flesh-warm booze was literally impossible for us to swallow, because we already knew what good drink tasted like, and we were young and healthy and had no need for extra stimulants. Other girls told us we must drink with our dates or have none, but we danced blandly past the Crash of '29 and into the Depression, learning a lot about the drinking patterns of our times, but always backed by what we had been taught unwittingly since our youngest days. There was good wine if we cared to look for it, or good beer-gin-whisky-brandy. And the best was none *too* good!

In 1929, I started to learn more seriously about winemaking and winetasting when I married and went to live in France, mostly in Burgundy, for three years. We were lucky to live there with the Ollagniers first and then the Rigoulots, who were as different as two middle-class French families can be but who shared a genuine zeal for learning how to live intensely. They used all their physical senses steadily and deliberately, like musicians or surgeons training their fingers, and they studied and talked and polished all their wits like artisans honing their tools.

When Paul Ollagnier, a municipal architect, had to inspect the attic beams in an old château down the Côte d'Or near Gevrey-Chambertin, for instance, he took us along, and we saw how to use the little silver *tâte-vins* and stand like polite awed sheep, in the cellars or courtyards, while the men went through their long obligatory tastings after the business at hand was over. The smell of ice-cold stone and wine and mildew was good. We were *learning*, with every cell and pore in our young minds and bodies.

On Sundays the Ollagniers took us on rough endless walks with the Club Alpin, and we ate and drank our ways through endless enormous meals in village cafés that seemed to live for our annual treks, and then we snoozed for endless train-rides back to Dijon and bed and the next week's classes. And all week we discussed with the family the dishes and wines we'd absorbed on Sunday, as if they were Corneille or Voltaire or the *futur indicatif* of the verb "to understand."

M. Ollagnier had a cousin in Belley in the Ain, who occasionally sent him a gamey pâté or some long-necked bottles of pale rosé or straw-wine from his vineyard farm, so I learned about Brillat-Savarin's country and started then and there my "continuing delight" in that old man's good company. I read the Ollagnier copy of his *Physiology of Taste* and was as surprised then as I still am that few Frenchmen knew of it.

And then the Rigoulots rented us along with the Dijon house and for many more months taught us a completely sensual and almost hectic approach to the pleasures of the table, as compared to the more academic detachment of the architect and his pianist-wife.

We ate too much and too heavily and drank fine bottles every day instead of on Sundays, as we hurtled with the passionate, desperate people toward their family ruin and then World War II. They had once been very rich, with a fine cellar, mostly of Burgundian and Alsatian vintages, and by then my husband and I knew more about what and why we were drinking. The good bottles and the delicate fine dishes and all the urgency of disintegration mixed into a strange dream for a time. What is left is sometimes sad in my heart, but always good, *sans reproche*.

Back again in California, there was the end of Prohibition, a forgotten blight while we'd been away. There was no extra money anywhere, so the new watery beer and the dregs of bootlegged booze were easy to forego. Now and then a few of us would "chip in" for a gallon of young but decent red wine, and eat bread and maybe cheese and talk all night, and plan glowing beautiful exciting futures as the jug emptied. We never felt like clichés-in-Time, which of course we were, politics and poverty and gallantry and all . . .

And since my first years and Father's sure insistence that there could always be good wine if it were looked for, I have found it and not bothered with anything else. By now the skill of growing and making it in California has progressed so far that I feel more secure than ever in my lifelong pursuit. Of course there will be shoddy bottles forever, because of the shoddy men forever born to fill and market them. But they cannot harm me, because I have never stopped learning how to tell the true from the false, with at least six of my five allotted senses. Any good winemaker keeps on learning, too, and this collection of some of the reasons for doing so, and the ways devised to assure that, would give heart to my own first teacher, Rex.

He took a dim view of Brotherly Love, the Immaculate Conception, and Prohibition, according to critics as disparate as my mother and the County

Boxing Commission, among others. He smoked cigarettes, mostly hand-rolled with Bull Durham, and pipe-tobacco until he lost his bite with dentures in his late years. He probably downed more than his share of drinkin-likka, as a newspaperman. He should have had a palate like well-tanned buffalo hide. But I never saw him smoke when honest wine was nearby, or falter in his first long silent appraisal of it, whether he was in a rancher's dim barn up in the California foothills, or in a Swiss vintner's cellar, or in a fine restaurant anyplace.

He was not my only teacher in this "appreciation course" that I shall continue to attend as long as I am conscient, but certainly he was the shaper, the power behind what I always feel when I know that I am drinking a good wine and that I may soon drink another. *Prosit*, to him and all such mentors!

1984

The Unprejudiced Palate
by ANGELO PELLEGRINI

In 1984 I did an afterword for The Unprejudiced Palate, *which was published by North Point Press.*

My sister and I found ourselves, one morning, in a ghastly Japanese-American restaurant in Los Angeles, trying to make some breakfast-sense with the editor and publisher of the Press. The professional bash the night before, which had dragged us out of our cozy Northern California enclaves, had been arduous emotionally but hardly worth bothering about gastronomically, and the four of us were starved.

Unfortunately, the Japanese-American idea of breakfast was almost as formidable as the fancy parties and banquets that had preceded it, and in a kind of desperation as we tried to smile over cold canned peaches and the Oriental idea of ham and eggs, we talked nostalgically of books that we'd like to read again, to take our minds back and away.

And the first one I thought of, for reasons that plainly had something to do with my current distaste for anything less than some crisp Italian bread and some fuming coffee with plenty of hot milk in it and maybe a dash of grappa, was a book that I had first read in 1948, by Angelo Pellegrini. For the long time since, I had felt refreshed and nourished and truly comforted by it. And then and there, as the four of us sat trying not to show our basic inability to eat or drink what was set before us, it was decided that North Point Press would get Pellegrini's book back into circulation as soon as possible. Just thinking about it made us feel better, and by the time we wandered out to our various cars and planes and so on, to head north again to more familiar grounds, all was well.

The afterword I wrote when I got home was easy to do. I felt almost as if I had said it all before I ever read the book, but of course this was impossible. The hardest part was to keep it from being a kind of love letter to Angelo himself, and I assume that this real affection is as obvious to any reader as it is to me.

He came down from Seattle, Washington, where I think he is emeritus now at the university, with his wife, Virginia. She is a tall, upper-class American with beautiful white hair, not at all the sort of life-companion one would expect an Italian peasant-refugee to choose, much less stay with for his whole life. She liked me and I liked her. We all went to lunch with the North Point Press people and had a fine time. Angelo, used to being pampered and petted and listened to, would stand up in the restaurant, tap loudly on his glass, and talk or rather expound. Of course, the other customers in the place were astonished but amused . . . we were a perfect captive audience, willy-nilly. It was fun, and I loved every bit of it.

We'd met here first, and had a drink of wine, and then after lunch we all came back and drank more wine and a little brandy and talked a lot. I hope it will happen again: Angelo and Virginia and I are carissimi . . .

AFTERWORD

Although I have known very few men of letters intimately, excluding my husbands, of course, Angelo Pellegrini is the only one I have ever shared a spit-bucket with.

Perhaps the nearest I ever came to this was one noontime in a heat spell in New York, in about 1944, when I waited a long time for Somerset Maugham to get up from his luncheon rendezvous with a handsome blonde and then sat as soon as possible on his chair. It was warmer than the weather, almost hot from his plump old bottom, and I felt it voluptuously through my whole being, like fine tea or perhaps a noble Chambertin sat upon and in, rather than drunk as common mortals would absorb it.

And sharing a bucket at the Pomona County Fairgrounds with Angelo Pellegrini, in about 1948, was even headier . . . or perhaps I should say soul-shaking. He detested me.

It was at the Los Angeles County Fair in Pomona. To please an old good family friend, Harold Richardson, I had agreed to be one of his crew in the first serious public wine-judging south of Sacramento, from whence had come all our official vinous nods until then. Of course we were frowned on, by anyone south of Santa Barbara, for stepping on hallowed tradition, but Harold felt that the time was right, and he asked a mixed lot to meet with him at the fairgrounds "down south." I was the only female there, and in fact the first of my sex ever to be on a California wine panel, as far as I know.

Of course it was very hot in September, and I dressed for coolness and changed my usual personal habits only by cutting out all soap and toothpaste and lotions and perfumes for two weeks; I did not smoke anyway, but I stopped any tea-coffee-wine-booze for five days before the judging. In other words, I was a Good Girl, a white Anglo-Saxon non-Christian.

The equipment for judging was very primitive then. For one thing, we were supposed to "do" about 180 bottled products in three days. For another, the "judges" were seated two-by-two at a long table with, of course, the bottles-on-hand and the spare glasses in front of each one and then a bucket, a plain old five-gallon bucket, between each pair. No dentist-office neat installations!

The first day we judged white wines. The second we whipped through reds. The third and final day we did fruit wines in the morning and brandies after lunch, and toward the end of that day we swallowed quite a bit, instead of spitting it hopefully toward our partners and fairly deftly into our shared buckets.

I had a hard time spitting in public, at first. I knew I would have to when I accepted Harold's invitation, because I had watched wine men do it nonchalantly in Burgundy and Switzerland. But they were always *men*. I had never seen a woman do it, probably because they never went into the courtyards outside their husbands' wineries when anyone was there. I did not count as a woman there, being a foreigner and by nature invisible anyway. But in Pomona, when I had to spit like a man, facing my companion across the bucket and trying to guess what he thought of the wine we had just let swirl and unfold in our separate mouths, I was at first almost appalled at myself. I was nearing forty, and I had never done such a thing as *spit*, except in a closed private space, and alone.

My partner was Angelo Pellegrini. At least, that was what was marked on his card and announced in the sheet Harold had sent to each judge.

I admired Angelo very much, and felt awed that I would actually meet him at Harold's little gatherings. I reread *The Unprejudiced Palate*, and felt more strongly than ever that it was the first true statement I had yet read about living as it can and should be in the western coastal America that I love. It did not occur to me that I would have to *spit* in front of this Pan-like man. And for a while it looked as if I wouldn't.

I sat alone at my slot and pretended to taste a few white wines, and watched how my neighbors acted, and even learned how to eject the juices without dribbling, before Harold hurried in from his office with a short dark furious man fuming alongside. Introductions were impossible as Harold's replacement put us through our paces and we gradually got into our own rhythms of tasting, marking, moving along through the rows of unmarked bottles. Beside me Angelo inhaled and swirled and swished noisily, and spat contemptuously almost everywhere but into our bucket, our private shared spittoon.

He was plainly in a gigantic rage.

And at noon, after one of the most miserable mornings of my life, Harold told me that Angelo had roared into his office a few minutes before the judging started and had said that he would never consent to have a woman present at a wine-tasting, much less sit next to *him*. He swore in two or three languages and was noisy in every possible way. He was, in other words, an insulted Italian, than which . . .

Harold, in his own more decorous way, was furious at having his actions called whatever Angelo called them, and finally he assumed all his legal sternness and said *put up or shut up*, and Angelo agreed to sit by me for one day.

But after lunch he stormed into Harold's office again and said that he could not go on. He was leaving for Seattle *this afternoon*.

Harold, by now smooth and silky and in general the successful criminal lawyer trying his most important case, had no need to counterquestion his client to discover that not only was the person appointed as his fellow wine judge a female, but that she *smelled*. She smelled of PERFUME. She was plainly unfit to sit next to a highly qualified and respected wine man–author–*bon viveur*, a true American but also a living example of good Italian sensitivity and general machismo. "She must go," he said. "Or . . . *I* go. She stinks."

Of course all these stormings were a painful interruption to Harold's plans to direct and cosset and teach and in general bend his first selected jury to his enological will. It was his show. He was supposed to be out there leading his flock, not closeted with a wild-eyed sputtering Italian professor. It was probably self-survival that got him to seat Angelo beside me again, still unintroduced and openly sneering, but able to function as a wine *judge*. (Angelo still spat before I did, and in several directions, and never looked at me or spoke.)

After work that night, Harold took me to dinner and told me, as soft-voiced and gentle as always, that Angelo Pellegrini, the man I so admired for his vital literary style, said I smelled. "To me, you do not," Harold added firmly, and I told him of my ascetic preparations for his unprecedented panel of wine judges, and he smiled approval in his usual avuncular-paternal manner, and said something like "Carry on!" We finished our unusually dull meal, saltless-sauceless-wineless for our palates' purity and next day's scheduled REDS, and parted without visible tears.

It was a bad day, but at least Angelo was there the whole time. He never looked at me or spoke, but his spitting was spotless. Whenever Harold picked up our scorecards he smiled a little, because we seemed to be marking the same things about the same bottles . . .

The next day was the last, thank God. I had never lived through such a miserable experience. My female honor felt bruised by the dark unsmiling man sitting with such obvious impatience and distaste beside me, sharing the same horrid bucket for our public rinsings, sucking in his breath whenever I had to lean toward him so that I would not pollute his pristine taste buds with my stench. I prayed for patience to get through the fruit wines, through the raw brandies, and away.

When we went into the plain bleak room, the glasses and first bottles and buckets were set out, and we placed ourselves, but Harold and Angelo were not there. In about ten minutes they hurried in and almost ran toward me, so that I stood up anxiously: was it bad news about my little girls, my ailing mother?

Angelo, flashing a beautiful boyish giddying smile, bowed low over my hand, and kissed it passionately. Harold almost danced around us. Probably all the other judges, middle-aged respected medicos and tycoons and physicists, looked on with bemused patience, ignorant of our little drama, as Angelo begged me to forgive him for his cruel actions and Harold explained patchily but almost as passionately that Angelo's motel soap smelled, and therefore he smelled, and especially his hands smelled. *I did not.*

The rest is obvious. Years fell from my shoulders, and I was young, beautiful, desirable. Angelo was alive beside me, as only a healthy Italian can be. We spat in unison into the suddenly attractive puddle of fruit juice and water we shared, and a newspaper paparazzo from Los Angeles shot our jets meeting in midair just above the bucket. And halfway through the long last afternoon tasting of brandies we all began to *swallow*, and ignored most of the other rules, so that before we all parted after a fine meal of heavily spiced delicacies and plenty of our best bottles from the first two days, I was *carissima* forever, to the antic god of the Pacific Coast, Angelo Pellegrini.

I still am, with the full consent of his wife, and the tacit agreement of scores of other fellow females in every direction from Seattle. Now and then Angelo remembers me, and sends me a clipping of something he has written, or a picture of his prize pumpkin, or a blurred snapshot of a new grandchild, all askew but eminently handsome and healthy because they came from Angelo Pellegrini: from him, the great god Pan of this Western world.

1984

New American Chefs and Their Recipes
by LOU SEIBERT PAPPAS

This is plainly a preface done for a friend. Lou Pappas is to me a remarkably interesting person, and I also like her. What is more, she is a good newspaper woman, and it is much more to her credit than otherwise that although this book called New American Chefs *is obviously done as part of her job for the Peninsula* Times Tribune, *it still manages to be surprisingly interesting. And one of the best things about my working for Lou Pappas is that she understands exactly what I am saying in this apparently somewhat circumspect language!*

Of course, a person like me is often asked to write some sort of guff about new books. Most of them, and not merely by coincidence, are exactly the same type as this one. They can be and usually are both trite and predictable, and what makes things even more difficult is that when they are also written by a friend, it's hard to seperate detachment from personal loyalties.

With Lou Pappas I had no such worries. She's an expert craftswoman as well as a warm but level headed friend, and in her case there was no need for me to look for that "jewell in the toad's head," that one valuable recipe in an otherwise boring and useless collection. It was really not a question of my saying ho hum *one more time.*

What was even better, there was no dreadful need to pull some faintly ambiguous words out of my timeworn old hat! This book about new American cooks is interesting and easy, and nothing to be ashamed of, and that is more than can be said about nine-tenths of such books now in print.

In other words, Lou Pappas has done a good book and I'm fortunate that I don't have to force myself to say so.

PREFACE

Perhaps this book about a young, fresh look at our ways of public enjoyment of the art of eating in America is an unwitting proof that we are all Peeping Toms!

What Lou Pappas tells us with seeming artlessness about the people who cook and own some of our best and most exciting restaurants makes us read the recipes they have sent to her as if we were gastronomical voyeurs. We learn where they came from, and even how they decided to be cooks instead of doctors or artists or nuclear physicists. Then we read her own generous hints of why they are good chefs instead of poor or piddling or plain bad ones (Who ever said that cooks hide their best tricks, and never betray the Secret Ingredient? Some two hundred recipes sent freely and even joyfully prove that old saw false . . .), and we snoop happily for *clues*. We feel as if we had a free codebook to their mysteries.

And as we enjoy the freshness of their skillful use of fruits and vegetables and even flowers that we had almost forgotten about during our long, enjoyable years of servitude to classical cooking, we realize that these new young chefs are not naive kids splashing around happily in a freak success. They are very serious, dedicated people, studying and training and practicing for a completely fresh way of leading us from trough to table.

All good cooks have always tried to, of course. They have used their skills and wits to make us feel intelligent, sensitive, well-fed creatures instead of hungry animals. Sometimes they have had to bow to the so-called progress of history, as when enjoyment turned to satiety in Greek and Roman and finally European cultures. Perhaps we, too, were in danger of this subtle takeover of gluttony in the last few centuries. In their cartoons Rowlandson in London and Daumier in France were not always flattering to the predominance of Pig over Puritan in our fairly recent public lives . . .

Of course this new wave of interest in food that is fresh and seasonal and local is far from original. But probably never before have whole parts of our planet's nations been as aware as we are now of the pleasures of looking at a plate of food deliberately planned to be attractive as well as delicious, and still be able to believe that it will nourish the whole person in us, the hidden hungry animal.

There are many of us who cannot but feel dismal about the future of various cultures. Often it is hard not to agree that we are becoming culinary nitwits, dependent upon fast foods and mass kitchens and megavitamins for our basically rotten nourishment. But one or two grudging peeks at what the bright, brave young cooks say, and at the patterns they have evolved and toss proudly and gaily out to us in books like this one, will do much to soothe our spirits. We will, I know for a fact, feel a new encouragement. We will arise from our next meal not so much "resigned," like the poet, as refreshed, and ready to head for further pleasure at both the table and . . . even *else-where*.

1984

wine with Food

A GUIDE TO ENTERTAINING
THROUGH THE SEASONS
by BARBARA ENSRUD

Wine with Food: A Guide to Entertaining Through the Seasons *was published in 1984 by Congdon & Weed, a good house that no longer exists. The foreword to it is by its own author, Barbara Ensrud.*

I wrote the little pre-foreword because I like and admire Barbara Ensrud, but I don't think I said very much in it. I did not do the serious job she and her book deserve. I would like what I said if I thought it gave things even a good cheering nudge, and perhaps it did. I wrote it with love and Barbara did too, because we both feel the same way about wine and food.

FOREWORD

Simple: Opposite of complex; straightforward
(Definition of word used in wine-judging,
Wine with Food, page 187).

This is, in more than one way, a good description of the book. It is also a good one of Barbara Ensrud's style, and of her subtle yet very uncomplicated approach to the whole overly fussy subject of marrying wines to dishes, and good drinking to good eating.

Books about gastronomy run in seasonal patterns; presently many of them are written as if winter, spring, summer, and autumn had been invented within the past two or three years for the sole purpose of making life simpler for writers about the pleasures of the table even though alphabets and calendars and even decades and centuries have been used mercilessly by many fine to dreadful scriveners in their efforts to justify "one more book" on the general topic of hunger itself. Inevitably most of these books will be forgotten, and rightly so.

Now and then, though, an attempt to explain our natural preoccupation with keeping ourselves alive and well and relatively happy seems meant to be read for a long time, and I think this book is one of them. I hope so, for good things should not be let disappear, and I feel that *Wine with Food* is written with skill and real honesty about something often murked over, today, by prejudices and affectations and plain snobbery.

But here and now, at least in Ensrud's book, the air is clear and sunny (or perhaps in winter properly cold, with a good hungry snap to it), and we can be as trusting as innocent children that what we eat will match to perfection what we are given to drink. (Of course, milk and hot cocoa go by the boards in this mature counseling, but once Bloody Marys are advised with complete rightness, to start a picnic or perhaps a tailgate booster, or where any wine would be impossible with the suggested food . . .)

Ensrud's sureness about this pairing is almost uncanny, at least to my own mental palate. Perhaps it is because I agree with her, most of the time!? Perhaps I like this book about what I would choose to drink with what I am eating because I wish I had said it myself!?

For instance, I like what she writes about rosé wines. She "keeps hoping" that here in our wine-rich country they will be made drier, and more simply, less pompously. We take rosés too seriously, she and I agree. It is as if the vintners are trying to pretend that rosés are indeed *not* "picnic wines" and certainly *not* vintage, but still not the good go-down-easy drinkin' stuff that they should be. And it warms my weary heart to hear such a firm clear voice as Ensrud's speaking out. We both know rosés well, and how they can be plain and still subtle, and sturdier than dry whites but never pretentious.

There are many other reasons for my liking this book and the personal but detached way the author has written it.

It is evocative, as all good reading should be. Once she says something about what to serve with the ceremonial turkey that is part of our traditional Thanksgiving, and I think at once of how my mother always insisted on serving a pale dry sherry with that hallowed bird, instead of the Johannesburg or bubbly that my father really preferred.

In other words, this book is not only helpful and reassuring, but it makes us think far past and beyond it, and I like that. Ensrud tells us that what we have already known will help us say yes or no to many of our future temptations and enjoyments, and that "given the chance" we can know even more! *Good!*

The Alice B. Toklas Cook Book

This foreword is for The Alice B. Toklas Cook Book, *published as a thirty-year memorial by Harper & Row, 1954–1984. They did a nice job. I loved writing the foreword. I think I got paid for it, but I don't remember . . . it was really a labor of love. Before my "foreword" is "a happy introduction" to the new edition, by S. M. Bessie, who did the first one thirty years before. The cover to the new book is well designed by William Graef, with a 1952 "Portrait of Alice" by Dora Marr on the front cover, and on the back a good shot of Toklas and Gertrude Stein in 1944.*

One rather amusing thing happened. There's a gay paper in San Francisco whose name I forget. Herb Caen said to me, "Do you know that you're now really one of the avant-garde of the Lesbian-gay set in San Francisco? It's because you got a wonderful rave review of the book." And I was pleased that it was not about me as a writer at all, but about the fact that I had written "a rarely understanding picture of one of the great marriages in Lesbian life." Herb was a little tittery about it, I thought, but of course he did not say anything about it in his column.

And that is the only thing I remember about this foreword, except that it was

indeed a pleasant job that I felt complimented to do. I do feel a little embarrassed
about some of my other introductions; they sound stiff and meaningless to me,
but this was a real job, because it was a good way to challenge my innately naive
honesty.

FOREWORD

What an extraordinary person! Miss Toklas has been an integral part of my
life (sensate, thinking, sensuous, spiritual) since I was in adolescence. And
when I was newly twenty-one and newly married, I could have met her.

My husband and I stopped in Paris in 1929 on our way to some three
years in Dijon at the university, and we had an "introduction" to Miss Stein
and Miss Toklas, but I could not bring myself to present it. I could not walk
around the corner with the letter in my hand.

Many years and lives later . . . and the fact remains that never did I meet
this strange person, except through what other people wrote and said about
her.

A while ago I reread *The Autobiography of Alice B. Toklas*, which the
Columbia Encyclopedia says Gertrude Stein published in 1933 "as if by her
secretary-companion." It is amazing, a literary tour-de-force, an almost
great writer going with almost surgical sureness into the self of a loved one.
It is amazing, because it feels and smells and is true; it is prescient. It is especially amazing for its detachment, its lack of vanity; it is not even condescending, the way a person is not condescending to his inner self. It is, for
the lover who was Gertrude and who can be me or any chosen soul, the
person who was/is Alice B. Toklas, and *no other*.

People who knew Alice or even met her casually—she often writes of
"friends (whom we had never met) of friends of ours"—always knew her
at once and forever, the way I did when I read her "autobiography," the way
Gertrude did when, a few minutes after she saw Alice, she said flatly that
they were married for life. People have told me that when this small ugly
woman was in a room they were keenly aware of her, before they even recognized her as Miss Toklas. She seemed to send out waves of inaudible
sound, like bells clanging somewhere in another space than ours. And since

I first read her so-called life, I am like everyone else, and know almost more about her and with her than I am really entitled to.

This was as true when I last lived in Paris as it had been the first time, in 1929, when I often walked past her door and knew she was behind it. By 1967 I had lived long enough to shed some of my first timidity, but she was hospitalized, too remote ever to welcome me as she might once have done.

I should perhaps try to explain how it happened that I missed my one last chance to meet her. In about 1938, my second husband and I were living in a vineyard south of Geneva, and we knew that now and then we must escape from our cautiously Calvinistic life as foreign landowners. We decided that we could afford, for a year or so, to rent two small rooms in the servants' quarters of the old Hôtel Continental in Paris, high in the attics about the Tuileries. We could leave books there, and perhaps some pictures, and city clothes. In the cold winters we could go up to *La Capitale*, escape the colder, duller, more structured life in Chexbres, feel warm and free before it was time to start spring planting and vineyard work . . .

Death and war changed all that.

But when I was offered a summer job in France by Time-Life, more than twenty years later, I took it. I felt I must go back, and this was my chance to. I was scared about being in Paris alone, for the first time in my life. I'd been there countless times before, with parents, lovers, husbands, children. This time I was by myself, my *self*.

I asked to be lodged in the attic rooms my husband and I had planned to live in. By then they had become stylishly expensive, but thanks to the potent clout of my temporary employers I went straight from St. Helena, California, to the small, low-ceilinged cubbyhole we'd meant to use for our books, our workroom. Sounds arose filtered and thin through the one big window, and the thick green of the Tuileries in summer. And in the next room, where we had meant to sleep, lived a trespasser, a stranger who became my good true friend, an elderly writer named Janet Flanner.

I had for a long time admired Miss Flanner's masterly letters from Paris in the *New Yorker*, and at first felt some of the shyness that had kept me so long from presenting my letter of introduction to the two ladies around the corner on the rue de Fleurus. And there Janet was, in our private special room! And indeed she was *there*, with her plain typing table, one beautiful cabinet of inlaid *boiserie*, with a big fading garden bunch, roses or field flowers brought each weekend from her lover's country house, her little bathroom always hung with a drying elegant nightgown or some tiny high-style panties. There were perhaps a hundred books and no pictures, and her narrow bed made the little room seem almost austere, except for the hum of all Paris as it rose from far below, and the magnificent light that poured in and up from the Tuileries and the Seine and the Left Bank. (Not long after that summer, Janet had to move to another old hotel because the Continental was bought by a world airline, but she was never as truly "at home" as in the attic bedroom where once I had thought I would live forever.)

Janet was much spryer than I, but was used to deputizing her many disciples, so that I spent most of that summer happily puffing around Paris on errands for her, fending off her fans at concerts, sampling a new batch of Sancerre in a cool cellar under the Luxembourg, with an ancient vintner she had known for countless years. . . . It was fine, and instead of being alone and scared in Paris for the first time in my life, I was more alive and happy than I'd ever dreamed of, because of all the good people who had unwittingly prepared me for it. I felt strong with their strengths, so that the work I had to do for Time-Life, and all the wild errands and jobs Janet loaded on me, seemed child's play.

But there was one thing she refused flatly to let me help her with. She refused to let me join her. She refused to *include* me, even vicariously, when she went several times a week to the clinic in the suburbs where Alice B. Toklas lay like a sightless, speechless vegetable.

Janet said firmly and simply that I must not see her now. She said that Alice would refuse to let me come, if she could.

So I never met her. *Ever*, that is.

Almost every day I went with Janet to Fauchon or a couple of other fine pastry shops that made *napoléons* or truffles or *palmiers* that Miss Toklas had once approved of, and watched Janet pretend that she was not going to eat the little treats herself as she sat by the bed of her impotent old friend. Then we hurried to the *Métro* and I watched her run down the stairs on her stylish tiny feet, carrying her stylish tiny offering.

She had known Alice B. Toklas for decades, about as long as I had, but face to face, as I never would. She was filled with love, and with anger that her old friend must die poor and abandoned. I mourned for them both, and was glad that Janet would eat a dainty voluptuous tidbit as she sat faithfully in Miss Toklas's silent hospital room.

But how else would Alice have chosen to be, after Gertrude died in 1946? It is true that the years between then and her own withdrawal were full; some people said that she finally "came into her own" as a dynamic and important figure. This may have seemed true, whether or not there could have been some malice in it, and I know from several of her friends that she ran her life with spirit, and entertained well, and handled the increasing complications about Gertrude's papers and belongings with surprising skill, for a person who had spent most of her life as a willing shadow. Myself, I feel sure that she was simply proving that Gertrude Stein had taught her well about the art of survival, as one final and gracious proof of their shared confidence.

Of course I "know" exactly what Alice looked like, and so far have not seen a picture of her that matches my own inner ones. Most of them are timid about how ugly she was. She was probably one of the ugliest people anyone had ever seen, to draw or photograph. Her face was sallow, her nose was big or even huge, and hooked and at the same time almost fleshy, the kind that artists try not to draw. And she had a real moustache, not the kind that old women often grow, but the sturdy kind, which started when she was first going into adolescence. I don't think she ever tried to shave it, or have it plucked out or removed chemically or with hormones, as a woman might do today. She wore it unblinkingly, as far as I can tell, although of course as a person of unusual awareness she must have known that some people were taken aback by it. A friend of mine who admired her greatly, and often traveled with her in her last years, wrote that Miss Toklas wore her close-cropped hair, which stayed black well into her eighties, in bangs "faintly echoed by a dark down on her lip." This amuses me. It is typical of the general reaction to something that would have been unnoticed except for her obvious femaleness. Another friend said more aptly, or at least better for my own picture, that her strong black moustache made other faces look nude.

She had remarkable eyes, very large and lively, the kind that seem to send off sparks, that sometimes look glowing with an inner fire. Probably people who were intimidated at first by her fixed upon them with relief . . . that is, until they forgot their shyness in the deft, supple way she moved and talked.

She was a tiny person, not five feet tall, I think, and she dressed with a studied daintiness, except for the clunky sandals on her pretty feet. They were almost an affectation, and almost offensive, the kind that Raymond Duncan and his followers wore as they ambled along the sidewalks of the Left Bank, unnoticed except by awestruck tourists. They wore togas of handwoven wool or cotton, depending on the weather, with thongs crisscrossed up their bare legs from their open sandals, and Isadora's brother always strode a few paces ahead, with a twinkling Cartier wristwatch on the arm that wielded his long shepherd's staff. Of course young students imitated these Chosen Few, at least in footwear, but it was always funny to see the sandals on Miss Toklas, below her fastidiously tailored suits, her fine silk blouses, even her loose, beautifully sewn house clothes.

She loved dramatic hats, and after Miss Stein's death she wore them oftener in rare gaddings . . . big extravagant creations with feathers and wide brims, and always the elegant suits and those clunky sandals. Nobody has ever written, though, that she looked eccentric. Perhaps it was because of her eyes . . .

According to the *Autobiography*, she cooked and Gertrude wrote. And according to her own cookbook, written several years after Gertrude's death, she cooked what she remembered eating when she was a girl in San Francisco, because her friend was homesick for American dishes now and then, so that from the time they first settled into their apartment on the rue de Fleurus in 1910 they served their own kind of "soul food" every Sunday night. But Alice had never been a housewife, in our sense of the word, so that the ways she evolved her down-home dishes stemmed more from nostalgia than kitchen experience, and the longer she lived in France and hired cooks there, and ate there, the less recognizable her "corn pone and apple pie" became.

Of course Stein, who seldom skipped a good meal and knew thoroughly the pleasures of a well-tended palate, never boiled water, much less an egg, as far as is known. Her "secretary-companion" tended to all that, and her delicious food kept Gertrude's ink flowing for all their long life together. It is even possible that Miss Toklas honestly *believed* that she only cooked while

Gertrude worked, and at the end of her famous *Cook Book* she says that when she told two friends that she was going to publish one, "The first one gaily responded, How very amusing. The other asked with no little alarm, But, Alice, have you ever tried to write? As if a cook-book had anything to do with writing."

And Alice B. Toklas honestly did not believe that it does, or even that it can. Probably she would shrug, and smile with pity and disbelief, to find that the cookbook she put together for publication in 1954 would immediately be recognized and then be issued again and again. It is of course a curiosity, for many reasons, like the fame of many of the artists and writers who came to talk and listen and eat in the Paris apartment of the two strange ladies from America. Alice knew why all of them were there, especially Gertrude. But she herself never believed that she could ever be more than their attentive loving nourishing shadow.

And yet probably not even Stein herself would have been able to write of a person she observed in a friend's house, "Like many first-rate women-cooks she had tired eyes and a wan smile." Miss Toklas made comments about the people and the recipes in her book exactly as she talked, so that she felt that her notes were not worthy of being called writing, which was to her a life apart, mostly occupied by Gertrude, with a few lesser geniuses lurking behind her mammoth shadow. And after Gertrude died, Alice went on talking, fortunately for all of us!

According to her, the *Cook Book* was written while she was laid up for several months with hepatitis. Her naturally sallow face turned pumpkin-yellow, and while she waited for her insides to stop heaving and churning at the thought of food, she satisfied her emptiness by remembering better days, as when the two ladies chugged around France in their ancient Model T Red Cross ambulance called Aunt Pauline. In 1916, Stein was "a responsible if not experienced driver. She knew how to do everything but go into reverse. She said she would be like the French Army, never have to do such a thing." And Aunt Pauline hauled food and wood and the wounded men dauntlessly, always forward . . .

Later there was Godiva, so named because she came to them stripped of everything on her dashboard, naked as only a "two-seater open" Ford could be in France after World War I. And between her and the worn but willin' Aunt Pauline, the other ladies seemed to find good food at the end of every mission, wars or not. Tarte Chambord, saddle of mutton, peaches, grilled perch with fennel . . . Alice never really loved Godiva, but always admired her.

Once after the war the sturdy Ford carried the two ladies to Vence, where Alice spent long mornings in a friend's vegetable garden. "It takes a long time to gather enough very young green beans for eight to ten people," she found. Between the vegetables and the roses her mornings were full, and she said happily, "To me this pleasure is unequalled."

Godiva took them much further along in their good lives, and had what both the ladies felt was an infallible gastronomical nose for sniffing out fine country restaurants for them. She was at last retired, not as a revered, respected remnant of the First World War, as Aunt Pauline had been, but respected nonetheless.

Of course it takes more than a lengthy jaundice attack to make a decent cookbook, much less a minor masterpiece, and there is no doubt that plain loneliness after the death of Gertrude Stein, as Alice always refers to her, meant that time had to be filled, with the quiet rich dignity that the tiny old "secretary-companion" had always shown. So in 1954 she finished a delightful collection of memoirs, *Cook Book*, and then in 1958, to international astonishment, she agreed to publish another book about food, when she was well past eighty, *Aromas and Flavors of Past and Present*.

In those days editors were still gracious enough to confess to the sins and errors of their proofreaders, so that a list was often inserted in a nicely designed book, giving words that had been omitted and phrases that slipped past the copyreaders. The first edition of *The Alice B. Toklas Cook Book* has one of these quaint courtesies, listing ten errata, and I feel quite sure that the author herself dictated it. Only three are really important. The rest correct misspellings or direct that "Gastronomique Guide" be changed to "Guide Gastronomique." It was easier and cheaper to be finicky then than in 1984!

And collectors will always want this curious book for one omission caused by our American Puritanism, as well as for its good printing and its miserably inept illustrations: it could not print Miss Toklas's recipe for Haschich Fudge for legal reasons.

By now, of course, the sticky candy that sounds a little like chopped fruit balls that children make for their relatives at Christmas has become more like cookies or brownies, but always named for Miss Toklas and always made with marijuana. Her recipe, regretfully omitted in 1954 but reprinted in paperback in 1960, was contributed by her friend Brion Gysin, and calls for "a bunch of *cannibus sativa*" pulverized. This plant is common in Europe, Asia, Africa, as hemp, and Miss Toklas kindly says that "In the Americas, while often discouraged, its cousin, called *cannibus indica*, has been observed even in city window boxes."

I have never eaten one of our "Toklas fudge brownies," but am told they taste slightly bitter, depending on how much pot is put into them, and that (1) they are absolutely without effect and (2) they are potentially lethal. Her directions are more lyrical. She first says that "anyone could whip up [Haschich Fudge] on a rainy day," and continues, "This is the food of Paradise— of Baudelaire's Artificial Paradises: it might provide an entertaining refreshment for a Ladies' Bridge Club or a chapter meeting of the DAR. In Morocco it is thought to be good for warding off the common cold in damp winter weather and is, indeed, more effective if taken with large quantities of hot mint tea. Euphoria and brilliant storms of laughter; ecstatic reveries and extensions of one's personality on several simultaneous planes are to be complacently expected. Almost anything Saint Theresa did, you can do better . . ."

Was this Alice B. Toklas talking, or Brion Gysin? The chapter called "Recipes from Friends," which gives their later, much-distorted recipes, holds several other deviations from her way of stating things. They simply don't *sound* Toklas-ian. Mary Oliver of London, for example, gives a terse recipe called "Birthday Ice Cream for Adults" that really sounds dreadful, and I like to believe that Miss Toklas included it because she was fond of Mary Oliver. (One of my grandmothers was named that too, but as a teetotalling Irishwoman she would never have considered adding a cup of rum to anything.)

During the German occupation of France in the Second World War, food was austere at best, with milk, butter, and eggs almost unknown even in the country near Belley, where the two American ladies lived in precarious security. Meat was rationed: a quarter-pound a week per person. At best, they lived in what Toklas called a "protracted, even a perpetual Lent." And it was then that she did what people have always done in times of hunger: she betook herself to "the passionate reading of elaborate recipes in very large cook-books."

Often I have sent *Larousse Gastronomique* or an American kitchen bible like Mrs. Rombauer's *Joy of Cooking* to students working their way through college, or to men in prison, and they have nourished themselves in many ways from their printed rations. And I know now as well as I did thirty years ago that Alice B. Toklas's *Cook Book* would feed my soul abundantly if I could find no other nourishment, just as it would make me smile in the midst of sadness, and feel braver if I risked faltering. It is a good book, "abundantly satisfying, imagination being as lively as it is . . ."

1985

California Fresh
by THE JUNIOR LEAGUE
OF OAKLAND-EAST BAY

In 1985, the Junior League of Oakland—East Bay published California Fresh, *and I wrote a little introduction for it, mainly because I'm fond of Jean von LöbenSels, who is an "angel" for these hardworking young women who too often are dismissed as "poor little rich girls" in our characteristically American reverse-snobbery.*

It was fun to write with the p. l. r. gs. who did a beautiful job of collecting rather dull material. Later, they all invited me to lunch, and I went because Jean came up from Bakersfield, where she now lives. (Old California joke: "Who lives in Bakersfield?" Now I know!)

The book itself is handsome and still sells well, in large part because it is beautifully illustrated, and also because it is skillfully edited.

FOREWORD

A few decades or perhaps I should say a while ago I wrote what was then called an article, but is now called a piece, about a Junior League cookbook published somewhere in the Deep South.

I liked the book because it was what I recognized as genuine. I also thought it was sad and pathetic and truly funny, which I made very plain in my story, and the editors were dubious about publishing it because they felt that it might harm their so-called image. They finally did.

To my real amazement I got a lot of letters about the article, and they were all good. They, and by *they* I mean the Binkies and TDs and Beejos of the Junior League, knew that I knew them and recognized exactly what they and I were, in that social and culinary and even global scene.

Their book was very bad, or rather it was not very good. It was inept. I said so, which was one of the things that bothered the magazine. But *they* knew what I was saying, and they wrote to me and *not* the editors and told me so. I felt fine.

Now I can say I feel even better, for here is another Junior League cookbook, and I am almost unbelieving about how much better it is than the other one I read and criticized.

I know that Binkie and TD will understand this, and even Beejo, who as I remember submitted a recipe for what she called Guzzpatchee that was mostly mashed soda crackers in canned tomato juice with chili powder. (This was during the South Pacific or maybe the Korean business, when wives found themselves stranded in strange places like Santa Laguna.)

Of course all that was a couple of wars ago, at least. But now in *California Fresh* the children and maybe even the grandchildren of our Binkies have produced a handsome book indeed, well designed, well edited, and filled with good recipes that have been tested with the severity that real sophistication demands. In other words, we've all grown up since those dim days when almost any group of well-meaning females could put together a batch of favorite dainties for their "club budgets," and count on a captive audience to hand out money because Mummy (or young Ms. Manell) had her name printed under Fudge Brownies (or Guzzpatchee) . . .

I admit to feeling an almost maternal pride in this big step from naïveté to cool, poised expertise. Perhaps I have always been a little uneasy about my first gentle teasing of these young ladies in Miami or wherever it was. Or perhaps I am simply relieved to see that I too am better able to recognize the rewards of hard intelligent work!

Certainly we all knew, all the Binkies and I, that enthusiasm is forever. There is as much of it in *California Fresh* as there ever was in the old childish, awkward, lovable cookbooks we once bought and tried to forget as soon as possible. By now we know we'll get our money's worth! We'll read and use and finally pass along to Binkie's great-grandchildren this present proof of her own integrity: *California Fresh* is a *good 'un*!

1985

The sophisticated Traveler

GREAT TOURS AND DETOURS
edited by A. M. ROSENTHAL
AND ARTHUR GELB

I wrote "Afterword: The Way It Was, and Is," in 1985, for the biannual section in the New York Times *called "The Sophisticated Traveler: Great Tours and Detours." I did it because I like the editors. They paid me well. It was fun to do, and I enjoyed it.*

It's a nice little thing, I think. It's a purely nostalgic personal approach to a subject. And to anyone who has read this book it will be a little bit of a reminder of the letter I wrote—the love letter, really—to Maurice Chevalier in 1972, because it talks a bit more about Cassis, and the day we went down there.

AFTERWORD: THE WAY IT WAS, AND IS

Why is it that people refuse, or are unwilling, to go back to a place where once they have been happy? If you ask them, they will say that they do not want to spoil a beautiful memory, or that nothing can ever be the same (a wonderful thing can only happen once!).

Perhaps they believe they are being kind and complimentary, thus to imply a perfection that must remain unflawed. Actually I think they may feel afraid that they will be disillusioned, if indeed they have had to convince themselves that a privately dull or ugly event was indeed a glamorous one. Or they may suspect that they are less attractive than they wanted to be, or that the other people are.

This has puzzled me since I was twenty-one years old and first married.

My husband and I went from Dijon in Burgundy, where we were students, down to the fishing village of Cassis, for Christmas. I lived in a mist of clumsy passion and ignorant naive wonderment, and although I cannot remember a single word we spoke, almost everything else rings like crystal in my memory: midnight Mass, with fishermen playing wild, sad songs on oddly shaped hautbois and windy flutes, over the bleating of two sheep by the altar glittering with candles; a new human baby wailing in its modern cradle trimmed with blue satin bows and filled with Christmas straw; all the short square women dressed in black, with shawls over their heads. We felt shy and bedazzled later, in the bright hall of the Hôtel Liautaud, when the villagers gave us thick glasses of a sweet brownish *vin cuit* and everyone talked a very fast dialect as if we understood it well, and finally kissed us and cheered as we went up to bed. And ten thousand other happenings: They are yesterday and tomorrow for me.

Of course, I never thought of anything but a long full life with my love, but a heavy foreboding hit me about two years into this planned bliss, when he said firmly that we must never go back to the fishing village where we had spent our first Christmas. And a cruel mixture of disbelief and sadness filled me as I came to understand how thoroughly and firmly he stood by his conviction, that if people know real happiness anywhere, they must never expect to find it there again.

I did not like to argue, then or ever, but I did want to find out why, and his basic answer was that it was foolish to try to recapture happiness. When I told him that I honestly did not have the faintest wish to be the ninny of two Christmases ago (to "recapture" anything), he was deeply hurt, feeling that I had considered him a fitting partner in our ingenuous love, a fellow fool. Plainly I was out of my depth: I fumbled along about how beautiful the wild hills were, back of Cassis, and how good the wine was, and how much I had learned since then. It would be wonderful to see it with older eyes, I said. Impossible, he said in a pitying way, as if I could never understand the pain of being a truly sensitive poet driven forever from his former paradises by crass realism.

So that year I think we went to Nuremberg, and the next year Strasbourg and and and, but we never returned to any place we had been before, because once, according to his private calendar, we had been there. And in a few more years we parted. You might say that we ran out of places.

I remain astonished, and very puzzled. It was obviously impossible to find out why he felt as he did, and to understand it, because I did not, and I still don't. When I tried to tell him that I did not want to "go back," it hurt him that I had not recognized the bliss he had tried to give me. And when I said that of course we were not the same as we had been, he thought I was telling him that he was older, which indeed we both were, and that I was unhappy that we were, which I certainly was not. And so on. Yes, impossible!

Fear may be a reason for refusing to admit change. And why would anyone be afraid of that? It is as inevitable as death, or "the ever-returning roses of the dawn," or curdled milk. And what reasonable human being would want to see always with the eyes of a bewildered lovesick timid child, which I was in 1929?

Many years after I was told by my young lover that we must never go back, my sister Norah and her three young boys, and my two little girls and I walked over the high white stone hills above the little fishing port of Cassis, and I cried out, "There it is, exactly as it was! Nothing has changed!" And we ran down toward its quays feeling delighted and happy.

True enough, wisteria hung richly from the trellises above the fishermen's doorways, and newly washed jerseys hung bright against the blue and green and white walls. Tough bleached old boats moved up and down gently on the flat indigo water, and down the quay there was a sound of a pianola I remembered from some thirty years before. My heart pounded with delight, and I grabbed the hands of Johnnie and Anne. "It's all the same! It's exactly as I knew it would be," I babbled, and I gave a big happy whack to one of the old familiar rusted bollards that still stood like sturdy mushrooms along the quay.

And it was made of papier-mâché! It tipped over like a matchbox and rolled off into the dirty bay, and my sister and the children watched while, as I was told often and gleefully for several more decades, my jaw dropped like a startled puppy's and I seemed to stop breathing, stop being. And then we all began to laugh, which we still do whenever we think of that wonderful return to the real-fake-phony-true place.

Maurice Chevalier was remaking one of Pagnol's movies there—*Fanny*—and the whole village was a set, as much like Marseille of many years before as it could be made, and everyone was in a high giddy fever of participation, with the mayor and the priest talking together in the striped sunlight of the main café terrace with some of the stars and grips, and people laughing as much as we were, if for different reasons.

My sister knew about my lasting puzzlement at my first love's firm refusal to go anywhere that had been happy for him, and we talked about it as we watched our five kids melt into the little gangs of actors' and fishermen's children. We sat under the paper wisteria in front of a fake café at the edge of the main set and watched one of the actors get out of a very ancient limousine countless times, for the cameras. Every take looked perfect to us, and every time the old actor creaked pompously from the backseat and stepped out, we smiled at his skill and then waited for him to do it again.

And I doubt that either of us had ever felt much more contented, serene, reassured. Quite aside from being well and with our children and filled with various kinds of love, we were in Cassis, exactly as we should be at that moment in history and time. And Cassis was there as it had been for more than two thousand years, and as it would be as long as there was a fjord-filled coastline between Marseille and Toulon on the north shore of the Mediterranean.

I think I was the first of our family to be there, between the world wars, when my love and I went there in 1929. A young fisherman rowed us far into some of the coves to show us where the homesick German sailors from the submarines lurking in 1917 or so had climbed up the stony sides and painted their sweethearts' names on the highest rocks: HANS & ANNA . . . ICH LIEBE HULDI, K. *v.* G. We ate the yolklike meat of sea urchins that he reached down for in the still, dark waters, so still that we could hear a fish jump. We did not talk much, but the three of us liked each other, and for several more days we would call and wave and smile, along the three short quays of the village.

He might have been any of the older fishermen who stood about now for the cameras, so long later. They wore their grandfathers' baggy pants and stocking caps instead of Levi's and beat-up visored baseball gear, and the children of Cassis were blissfully arrogant as they strutted among the real movie kids and our envious five, in some designer's idea of how Marseille street brats dressed when Panisse ran his pub. One or two little boys had tried some makeup in their adventure as potential stars, and marked freckles over the bridges of their noses, like some blond, blue-eyed urchin they had once seen in a Hollywood movie. They looked touchingly improbable; dark-eyed descendants of the Greeks and Saracens never freckle.

But they were part of our private return. They had been there forever. And so had I. And I realized that the dear man who had first gone there with me had never really been there at all.

Where had he been, then? We'd eaten and drunk and made love, listened to the wild sad rejoicings of the Christmas midnight Mass together. Why did he fear to do it again?

Norah and I moved on down past the cameras and the serious village extras and the old actor getting in and out of his ancient car, and sat under the bamboo slats at the big café, talking and wondering. Lots of children came and went, and Mr. Chevalier came in alone and smiled tentatively at us, wondering if I wasn't somebody from the Paramount lot in Hollywood a long time before—as indeed I was. The white wine was cool and like delicate flint, as it had been even further years back. (Why had my love not wanted to taste it ever again, at least there and with me?)

Norah and I decided without words to stay by ourselves, and not smile back at the charming old actor, who looked suddenly lonely and wandered away. The children came along the quay with two American kids traveling with their movie parents and several locals, still exhilarated by their professional debuts as extras. They were incredibly rich at three dollars a day, even if their pay would go directly to their parents, but temporarily they were as broke as any proper thespian and consented graciously to drink a lemonade or two with us. The whole gaggle sat at the far end of the striped shade, like a scene from a child's version of *La Dolce Vita*. Norah and I looked remotely at them, and out into the afternoon shadows along the broad quays and the darkening water, and wondered how we could be anywhere but there, then.

I still think that first fine young man was mistaken. Perhaps his stubbornness was admirable, but his refusal to change his *idée fixe* was plain stupid, to my older, wiser mind. Who wants always to look at a café or an altar or an oak tree with the first innocence and the limited understanding of a naive lovesick girl, or a born-again Byron?

Five minutes or five centuries from now, we will see changeless realities with new eyes, and the sounds of sheep bleating and a new child's wail will be the same but heard through new ears. How can we pretend to be changeless, then? Why be afraid to recognize the baby in the straw, just because it is not as it once was, innocent, but is now tied about with nylon ribbon? Is it wrong to see the phony, painted mushroom-bollard on the quay and accept it, as part of the whole strong song that keeps on singing there, in spite of wars and movies and the turtling-on of time?

(There are other places to go back to, even after wars both inward and outward, and new eyes keep on being opened. Nuremberg, anybody? Cassis?)

1985

A Commonplace Book of Cookery
compiled by ROBERT GRABHORN

A Commonplace Book of Cookery *was collected by the San Francisco printer Robert Grabhorn some time ago, and was reprinted by Andrew Hoyem, his devoted pupil, in 1985. It is a nice little book of nothings, really, and writing a preface to it was a kind of vanity job for me, because I am admiring of Hoyem as well as his mentor.*

As such, it seems like a good way to end this collection of nothings that I've written about books by other people. At this point, the collection I've made seems silly to me, and yet it's been written over about twenty-five years of my life, and I see that now I do write more easily than I did at first. The impersonality of my review of my godchild's first cookbook is quite different from this last easygoing preface to Robert Grabhorn's equally easygoing collection of tidbits.

I also see an increasing tendency to be reminiscent. This is probably proof that I'm reaching what close friends sometimes call my "Anec-Dotage," mostly because my family calls me Dote.

Maybe this is a good way to end . . . although since the preface for the Grab-

horn job has fallen into order I'm already working on a couple more. There is no
real end to it, except to end me, which of course could happen at any time. Mean-
while, I'll stop in 1987 with Robert Grabhorn himself.

PREFACE

For anyone addicted to reading commonplace books, which are rarely compiled by commonplace people, of course, finding a good new one is much
like enduring a familiar recurrence of malaria, with fever, fits of shaking,
strange dreams. Unlike a truly paludismic ordeal, however, the symptoms
felt while savoring a collection of one man's pet quotations are voluptuously
enjoyable, as I have found lately with Robert Grabhorn's deep and tanta-
lizing book.

The usual fever is one of enjoyment, in recognizing old favorites and
familiar sentences I myself would certainly have included . . . if ever I had
got to the brutal point of making my own collection with dedication rather
than dawdling. And the shakings are based on both envy and shock, at what
Grabhorn often chose, and why this or that utterly valueless triviality clutters
his pages, and where he missed an extraordinary jewel such as I would have
tucked in. And the strange dreams, feverish and shaky, are naturally about
my own unwritten commonplace book, one such as never before has been
put together, a distillation of humankind's purest spirit, an intuitive (and
egomanic!) appreciation of all the wise wit of our centuries (and a lasting
monument to my own!).

Countless readers have fallen victim to this form of intellectual infection,
fortunately for the rest of us who realize that we could or should have suc-
cumbed, no matter how modestly and privately, but who were well dosed
instead with the quinine of ambition, or of social inertia. All we can be is
grateful, as we feverishly, shakily (dreamily, jealously, scornfully, delight-
edly) read what others have compiled, from their own long readings.

Mr. Grabhorn, who was born in 1900 and died after a fine full life in 1973,
did just such a job for the rest of us lazier lovers of what others have said
better than we could. (Envious as we are of the fellow sufferer who actually
got his compilation onto paper, we at least chuckle and sigh and agree . . .
most of the time.)

Robert Grabhorn began his clipping early, and during his lifetime collected at least eight volumes of quotations on printing alone, and the prospect of editing and/or reading them should raise the temperature of any press-paludist. He was about thirty, though, and well along in his rich life, before he began to pluck gastronomical crumbs from off and from under the tables of the great, sub-great, superficial wits and thinkers of History, and he did not stop this delicious habit until a few days before he died.

It probably began when his elder brother and printing partner, Edwin, sent him to Europe for a year, in 1923–24. Of course he studied bookbinding and observed presses and suchlike there, but he also worked diligently at the arts of eating and drinking. Then, back in America, he married the "brilliant and outrageous" Jane, with whom he zealously continued his full curriculum. She undoubtedly whetted his fever for collecting quotations that could stimulate or amuse or even irritate him (which is what most commonplace books are for, of course).

Plainly Robert Grabhorn used his clipping habit, subconsciously or not, but on every subject that interested him, as an educational tool. He had never graduated from college, but kept learning until he died, fighting jauntily with his self-forged weapons.

He and Jane, who at one point founded her own Jumbo Press to spoof all such fine printing as the Grabhorns turned out with intuitive taste and skill, made a firm custom of "going out" at least three times every week, to restaurants and night-spots. They were familiars of North Beach in San Francisco, which was even more intensely riotous in their time than it is now. They ate with insatiable enjoyment, drank plentifully and well, and never, or almost never let their roisterings interfere with the next morning's session, press-side.

Once, though, they missed a day's work, according to their friend Porter Garnett, the great printer-designer. He was disturbed not to find them at the offices, and went to their place on Russian Hill. There they lay side by side on their big bed, rigid and speechless with rage at each other. They had been either bowling or playing bocce-ball early in the morning on upper Broadway, they said in surly snarls. Bob had dropped a ball on Jane's foot. Then she had in some way (Garnett was a very discreet friend, especially about ladies) injured her playmate in retaliation. And there they lay, implacably not speaking to each other, not touching . . . until it was time either to hobble out again for dinner or welcome the floating population of thirsty hungry voluble companions who filled their nights at home.

An incident like this may seem to have little to do with Mr. Grabhorn's steady and perhaps stubborn compilation of his private commonplace books, all the while his presses were printing more than five hundred beautiful volumes. Myself, I do not think it is trivial. It is part of the reason for his choices of quotations. While he lay silent, bruised, and enraged, he may well have been choosing several new titbits for his little book:

> My soul is dark with stormy riot,
> Directly traceable to diet.

Samuel Hoffenstein said that, and it rang with new truth. And Alexandre Dumas once quipped profoundly about a bibulous absentee from a business conference,

> . . . he absinthes himself a bit too much . . .

and then H. L. Mencken observed all too cogently,

> No man is genuinely happy, married, who has to drink worse gin than he used to drink when he was single.

It seems quite probable to me that after a little more of this wry medicine, Mr. Grabhorn could give Jane a slap and a tickle, rise from his bed, and repair immediately to his desk drawer where the cookery collection hid . . . and that then he and his wife limped back to life, back to the presses . . .

Among the several reactions to a good commonplace book of anyone infected with the virus, few are truly negative, and the meanest of us is genuinely delighted when a special quotation has made the grade in another man's book (as I was when I saw an inimitable line from Daisy Ashford's *The Young Visitors* just where I would have put it in the Grabhorn . . .). But probably the best thing about such shared reading is the relationship with the one who made it possible, the one who did the clipping, the sorting. It is not presumptuous, but it is usually personal and even intimate.

I never met Robert Grabhorn or Jane or Brother Edwin, but I have long been aware and appreciative of what they did for printing and fine publishing in the modern world, and through mutual friends I have relished stories of their vigorous lives in and out of the pressrooms. And now, cheated by both Time and Circumstance but rescued by Robert's consuming fever for the written word, I know him well! He garnered what I too would have, given his lusty curiosity and lack of sloth, about fingerbowls, sauerkraut, garbage, milk and Scotch and wine and beer and even Temperance, eggs, teeth, politics, cocktail olives, poverty, garlic, remorse and love. . . . Plainly he was a man of more than our common spiritual grace and good humor, and a good one to know, then and now.

part two

Introduction to Part Two

Perhaps it is arbitrary, but certainly it is easier to put my own introductions and conclusions and forewords and afterwords in one little chronologically ordered clutch, which I now do, than to cope with each one separately. I don't need to say that it seems impossible that I actually wrote all this stuff, but I suppose the proof is in the printing thereof. (Another handy adage states that "There's no fool—," but I have no time to waste in finishing it!)

And perhaps I should make the firm statement here and now, and probably for the last time, that I have never read what I have written, in whole, although sometimes lately I have lapsed for a page or two, in part. This peculiarity has been called everything from egocentric to plain sick, and of course it is nothing to boast about, but it is the truth. I myself suspect that it is self-protection that has made me shun reading what I've written, once it is in print: it's always painful to admit that what is done is done. *It's out, then it's gone . . .*

Fortunately, I've always been able to correct my own first drafts with an almost frozen detachment, and even more fortunately, I've had very little of that to do. This is partly because of my nature, but mostly because of my longtime training as a journalist. When I was fifteen or sixteen I was being deputized by my father to substitute during vacations for the Society Editor, the Gardens and PTA man, and even the Sports Editor. It's lucky for me that this was in the summertime, when almost nothing happened in Whittier. I learned in my early days, if I had not already known it through my cells and bones as a fifth-generation newswriter, that there's never time to rewrite and to consult the dictionary and to brood or ponder.

Father's paper went to press at three in the afternoon, six days a week, and my stuff had to be on the copy-editor's spindle by one at the latest. So all the time that I was sharpening pencils for the older reporters, and running across the street to the dairy for a pint of milk for my father, who more often than not unthinkingly poured it into his wire wastebasket when he thought nobody was looking (a mess, every time!), my mind was shaping sentences and learning without even knowing it to punctuate, and even to think, as naturally as I breathed.

And that is why I think that there is nothing much better than working on a newspaper to break any loose habits a wishful writer might form about doing one sentence twenty-six times before it is perfect. (I was once told that Ernest Hemingway did this, but I refused to believe it . . . perhaps a paragraph now and then, yes; a sentence, even a long one, no.)

So, except for one ugly experience, I was never made to reread anything I had written. Once I went for a while to a psychiatrist in Beverly Hills, and early on in our work together he asked me what I thought of what I wrote, and when I said I never looked at it, he said in real amazement, "But that is sick!" So I agreed to read a few pages of anything I wanted to, and I think I picked up The Gastronomical Me *and got to about page eight before I was forced to run to the nearest bathroom and throw up . . . dark spots swimming ahead, and wambly legs, and of course a violent gut reaction. So the next time I saw the doctor I told him with embarrassment what had happened, and he looked at me with even more astonishment and said, "But that is* sick!" *"Yes, I certainly am," I said, and we agreed that I would never have to do it again.*

And the other day, almost fifty years later, I picked up a copy of A Cordiall Water *to see if there was a cough remedy in it that my mother had told me about, and there was, and I read several pages of that and then went on to the story of my wonderful cat Blackberry. Suddenly, I realized that I was quite enthralled. I was swept along. I loved it.*

Even writing this makes me feel sheepish, because I think now that instead of pecking away at old copies of Ellery Queen's Mystery Magazine *and old and new books that fall into my hands, perforce, I'm going to read something I've written. This is an odd thing to admit, after so long and rigid a deliberate ignorance. But even as I write of my new resolution I begin to doubt that I will carry it out. Why risk disturbing my present bland self-deprivation? I can always be comforted with the memory of the first review of a book I got. It was printed in a fairly obscure Chicago paper and was by a young reporter named S. Hayakawa, of later senatorial renown, who said absolutely everything kind and good and perceptive and sensitive about my first book,* Serve It Forth. *I decided right then never to read another review, and I have stuck to that vow fairly well. Of course, now and then, I take a peek if some dear friend tells me of an especially snide or dreadful one, and I always write nice little thank-you notes to reviewers, both pro and con. But Mr. Hayakawa summed it up as exactly as anyone could hope, so why go on reading other people's views and reviews, from about 1937 until . . . ?*

I honestly don't believe that I ever thought of publishing anything, although I wrote as naturally as I breathed from about nine, when I almost but never finished my first novel. I don't think I ever dreamed of signing *anything, or having a byline . . .*

It was all the work of people who felt they were being kind to me . . . "encouraging" me. If I had in turn been ambitious, or had in any way dreamed of being a writer, I would say that I got one big lucky break at the very start. And the start, as I try to look back that far, was the fault of Dillwyn Parrish, but long before it occurred to either of us I would be his ever-loving wife before he died in 1941.

Dillwyn, called Timmy, lived with his wife Gigi for a time in Laguna, next door to my husband Al Fisher and me, during the Depression when nobody we knew had a job. The Parrishes at least had money to pay their rent. Al Fisher and I lived in a house that we kept tidy for three winters for my family to come to on weekends. We were good friends with Gigi and Timmy, and later when we all moved to Hollywood and Occidental College and other jobs, we continued to see as much as possible of each other. And when I began to write little bits of description of some of the books that were left on the table beside me in the public reading room of the Los Angeles Library, to entertain my husband, he showed them to Timmy. As I remember, this annoyed me a little because I had no idea they were for any eyes but my dear husband's. And Timmy sent them to his sister, Anne Parrish, who was a famous novelist. She was apparently pleased enough by them to send them to her editor, Gene Saxton of Harper & Brothers, and he in turn gave them to Hamish Hamilton in London, and the jig was up. Whether I liked it or not, I was doomed, condemned, set.

Of course, I am glad that I was, because there is nothing else I do at all well except perhaps cook or write letters. (And even these two virtues are strictly selfish: I cook to please my friends and I write letters so that I will get replies! Possibly I write because it makes me feel better than anything I know except perhaps good love-making, to finish a book and be ready to start another . . .)

So, in 1936, when I was in London, Hamish Hamilton and Gene Saxton invited me to tea in the publishing-house offices, and I felt shy but knew that I was well-dressed and in fact probably as dashing as I ever had been, since I had just come over from Paris with a new hat and shoes. The two men looked at me with utter horror. In fact, I've never been so glared at by such sick-faced fellows in my whole life.

I stood there in the doorway until Gene Saxton finally tottered toward me, and they both began to tell me in very weak voices that I could not possibly be M. F. K. Fisher. When I asked them why not, because it had seemed perfectly natural to me to sign my name with initials for the first three words just as my mother signed her own E. O. H. for Edith Oliver Holbrook Kennedy, they replied that no woman could possibly have written Serve It Forth. *But I had! And I was a woman! Finally, they admitted that they had planned to be rather toplofty with a frail young don from Oxford or perhaps even a yearning clerk at Sotheby's or Christie's, but never a dame like me. Gradually they grew used to the shock of my obvious femininity, and by the end of the long teatime we were planning fairly intelligently how best to get around the cold fact that nobody would believe that* Serve It Forth *had been written by a woman.*

And the first time around, few people did. In fact, few people read the book at all, although it was touted as a "Harper find." I remember nothing else about it except for the perfect review by Mr. Hayakawa, and a short note from Alfred Knopf, telling me he wished that he had published Serve It Forth *and hoped that some day . . .*

There is no real introduction or afterword to this book, which perhaps proves how naïve I was when I wrote it, but I did write two little things I timidly called "To Begin" and "To End." I dedicated it to my father and mother, but I don't think they ever mentioned it to me, although I'm sure that Mother must have glanced at it.

And this reminds me that it has always been almost a joke in my family, the disregard they've shown toward anything I've ever written. Once, at dinner, after four or five books had been published, I asked my father if he had had a chance to look at the last one, and he seemed bewildered and said, "Edith, didn't we have a copy of that around?" And suddenly I was so angry that I banged my hand down on the table, and I remember that we were drinking white wine that jumped in all the glasses, and for the first or second time in my life I said, "God damn it!" Everything stopped. I went on rather lamely, "You all act as if I had tertiary syphilis whenever a book comes out!"

There was a pained silence, and then Father said exactly as if I were about twelve years old, which indeed I had been the last time I heard The Words, "Mary Frances, you may leave the table!" Of course I did, but being more than twice twelve, I soon came back and apologized to everyone, and sat down again. But the silence still rang about my being in print, and by now I know the reason.

It is because I am indeed a journalist by birth. My own father probably wrote an average of two thousand words a day, six days of the week, for a good sixty years of his life, and I doubt that he was ever complimented in any way for this real feat. What is more, he would have been startled and embarrassed to hear his daily stint mentioned. And his father had been the same, and his mother too, and on back for another hundred years or more. And by now I know that although my loyal fans may tell me kind and reassuring things about my work, I will never hear anything but an occasional taciturn mention from my family.

I was cut out to write, though, and willy-nilly, and in 1941 I published a small book called Consider the Oyster, *an odd book without foreword or conclusion, which I had written to amuse my husband Timmy. I remember that I wrote a sad little criticism to my new editor, Sam Sloan, of Duell, Sloan & Pearce, about how I wished that I'd been notified earlier that the book would be published, because neither Timmy nor I knew about it and I very mistakenly felt, for a few minutes anyway, that he might have put off dying, if he'd known the publication date. As it was, he never saw the book, which was small and short. I dedicated the book to him, and I began to realize then that I must always write toward somebody I love, to make it seem real.*

That same year, 1941, I wrote a book called How to Cook a Wolf. *I did it in a few days, it seems to me now, as I walked up and down in Timmy's studio and dictated it to my sister Norah, who took it onto the typewriter. She was astonished by the smooth way it came out. I was still in strong grief and was beyond any feeling of surprise; it seemed quite natural to do a good book exactly as I would do a good report for Father's paper, to earn my living in the only way I could. This was probably the first time I was aware of writing to pay my way, and it may have helped keep everything so clear and fast.*

For some reason the book was sold to World Book Company—probably because Duell, Sloan & Pearce had already published Consider the Oyster *that year. And because it was wartime and we were beginning to feel the pinch of rationing and comparative isolation, with their resulting lack of luxury foods, the book was an immediate success. I think it was even called a best-seller in some parts of the country. (In 1951 I did a revised edition of it to make it more of a postwar helper, and that time I wrote the introduction and conclusion I include now.)*

The book was dedicated to Lawrence Paul Bachman, who gave me its very catchy title one time when he was trying to convince me that I should not live alone on my empty ranch. We were coming from an interview, I remember, with the artist-designer Charles Eames, who rightly felt that there was no place at all for me in his scheme of work. Larry said, "You must not live alone at the ranch. Take any job you can get. Or write a book. Or do something." So first I wrote this book, and then, after its phenomenally fast production, I did indeed do something and took a job in Hollywood.

In 1943, Duell, Sloan & Pearce published The Gastronomical Me. *It's a very personal book, and since my first attempt to read it for the psychiatrist I've never even looked in it. I do, however, recognize the first paragraph of the foreword as something that has been quoted, now and then: "People ask me: Why do you write about food, and eating and drinking? Why don't you write about the struggle for power and security, and about love, the way others do?"*

The Gastronomical Me *was dedicated to my sister Anne Kennedy Kelly, who was two years younger than I and always a complex and fascinating person. She died in 1965.*

These first five books about food were collected in 1954, and published by Donald Friede for World Publishing. He did not do this just to please me, he did it as a good publishing gimmick, which indeed it was. I remember that the book cost its readers the enormous sum of $6.50, and it was always made clear in the publicity that it was a good bargain, because that price covered five complete books by Fisher, who was beginning to be recognized as a minor authority on what the title somewhat pretentiously called The Art of Eating.

Since the first hardcover appearance, the book has been sold, first to Macmillan and again and then again to various publishers on both sides of the Atlantic, and just lately was bought by a Japanese firm. It is commonly assumed that because it is still in print and selling well, I am at least a millionaire. There is no such danger. There are too many fingers in one pie—thanks to the fact that the whole thing started out with old material, and with each book having its own agents and publishers and so on, plus my own three or four good agents—for everyone to take more than a little cut each time a new edition is brought out.

Fortunately, this is of no concern to me, and I continue to be pleased that it sells. By now I am quite used to having the granddaughters of some of the Wolf's *first readers, especially the war brides who depended on even the most dreadful recipes in it, write to me of how reassuring they have found something I've written. This is, quite literally, heartwarming.*

When The Art of Eating *was first published in England, some snafu limited it to only four of the books: the Duell, Sloan & Pearce edition of* How to Cook a Wolf *could not appear then in the U.K. I was really distressed. If anyone needed some information about how to cook the wolf at their door, the poor Limeys did!*

All five books are now included in a British edition, and mail continues to be approving from there, which is gratifying; there are too many dear people on my list in Wiltshire and in Scotland whose diets could use my little bits of economical savvy. Of course, some of my shortcuts make me wince now, but I know that ration cards and other strictures of war-time do strange things to human power, and I am not too uncomfortable that some of my ghastly recommendations are still being followed between wars by some otherwise fine people. I know that not only my intentions but the instructions are trustworthy, if unappetizing. (Perhaps here I'm thinking of a dreadful recipe called simply Warcake . . . or have I dreamed this?)

In 1946 I made a kind of anthology called "A Book of Banquets," Here Let Us Feast. *I had married Donald Friede and had changed both publishers and agents, so that Pascal Covici of the Viking Press was my new editor, and instead of Mary Leonard Pritchett, who had seen me well through my first books, I was taken care of for the next thirty-eight years or so by Henry Volkening. All this happened because of my new husband, a dynamic and restless person who knew almost as much about publishing as he did about modern art and other forms of seduction. He and Pat Covici had once been the meteoric team of Covici-Friede, which published more Pulitzer and Nobel Prize winners in its short years than* most publishers ever set eyes on. Donald was a great help in my rather innocent approach to this "Book of Banquets."

The book was amusing to do. We had a summer lease on a duplex down on Bank Street in the Village. Every morning I walked in the cool bright air to Fifth Avenue, where I either went on walking, or rode on top of one of the grand old buses, to the Public Library. I would work all day in the big reading room, with lunch often at exciting places, and then a late afternoon glass of white wine in the gardens of the Museum of Modern Art while I waited for Donald. We would walk or ride in the breathless summer twilight, to dine with people in their high apartments or down in the Village in the sidewalk restaurants. The whole long summer was a dream of hard work and hard play, and it ended as all good things must when we returned to the ranch in Southern California for some more years of work and play.

It was not until I revised Here Let Us Feast for a new edition by North Point Press in 1986 that I realized how warped by Prohibition so many of the well-known writers of the first half of the century had been. I found myself chopping out whole excerpts that had seemed essential twenty years before . . . so many bootleggers, so many hangovers, so much half-drunken repetition in what I had once read with real pleasure, by Sinclair Lewis and Thomas Wolfe and all those good people! And things that I never cared much for, anyway, I found easier to cut away, since my dear husband was no longer alive . . . excerpts from Pearl Buck for instance, whom he admired very much and who was one of his prize clients when he was a literary agent.

There were a couple of other things that fell before my sterner eye, in the revised anthology: I chopped out with real regret, for once, a poignant episode from Booth Tarkington's Alice Adams. It hurt me to do so, because it is completely true, and hopeless, and Midwestern. But it was written in a flat style or lack of style that shocked me much more than it had when I first included it.

This pleasant book of mine, which I'm glad to have available once more, mainly as a nudge to people's memory for things that they really want to read again, I wrote for my younger sister, Norah Kennedy Barr.

In 1947 I produced something that I did not want to do, as I've explained in the afterword to Not Now but Now that I tacked onto it when it was reprinted by North Point Press in 1982. Pat Covici of Viking, and Donald Friede, who was still my husband then, convinced me that I must write a novel. The Viking edition had its usual poor sales and Donald had to admit that I was indeed not *meant to be a best-seller, and certainly was not destined to make money in Hollywood. Until that moment, he had refused to believe me when I told him that I was blackballed there because I had broken my contract at Paramount, with the help of the Screenwriter's Guild, just before I went to New York. Whether or not this blackball still holds for me, I'll never know, and I have never cared.*

It was probably this last fact that remained a mystery forever to Donald. Even so, I dedicated the non-novel to him, with undying admiration and affection.

It was fun, that summer of 1946 in New York, to meet all the people of the various publishing sets as a callow Westerner. I made a lot of mistakes, all of them by accident, but I was well received by the sophisticated people I was suddenly playing with. It was just after the war, a strange time indeed, and New York was filled with glittering bitter refugees. I promised to do a book for Pat Covici about a similar time in Switzerland, when Geneva and all the little villages around the Lake swarmed with brilliant refugees from France. Mme Récamier and Mme de Staël had their salons, then, and Brillat-Savarin flitted around the edges before he headed for the more golden shores of America. It was fascinating, but I could not find the heart for it, after that summer, although I did start my translation of The Physiology of Taste, *which George Macy published in 1949.*

The Physiology of Taste *is a beautiful book, illustrated by Sylvain Sauvage as his last work. It was done for the Limited Editions Club, and of course was a costly volume; it now sells for many times its original members'-price of twenty-five dollars, high in those days. The same edition, but much less elegantly bound and not boxed, was printed for the Heritage Book Club at the same time and cost five dollars.*

George Macy stipulated that after his death his wife, Helen, not dispose of any of the plates of his really remarkable output, but various pressures wore her down and she and her son consented to sell the book, but not the drawings, to Alfred A. Knopf, who republished my original translation in 1971. It was later published by the paperback division of Harcourt, Brace, Jovanovich, since Vintage-Knopf did not feel it was profitable enough for them.

It seems odd that I continue to speak of it with such apparent conceit as the best translation available in the English language, but I know without any cavil that this is true. I'm equally aware that before long my translation will sound as odd and archaic as does the original French, and that a newer and better one will come along. This is as it should be. It pleases me that whoever has the next try at this will have my translation to refer to rather than any others I have read. They are scholarly enough, but sadly inadequate and at times guilty of the very British trick of snickering and tittering when what the old French lawyer really called for was a good smile . . . even an occasional belly-laugh.

I wrote a translator's preface for George Macy, and then a postscript, and I am as honored today as I was then to find my name in the same book as Brillat-Savarin himself.

In 1949 I also published another book for Pat Covici, An Alphabet for Gourmets, *most of which had already appeared in* Gourmet *magazine. I've always been pleased by the strange little drawings Marvin Bileck did for it. I dedicated the* Alphabet *to Hal Beiler, who had been my doctor for a long time, and who kept a kind and loving eye on me for another twenty-five or thirty years.*

Then comes a seeming lapse in my productivity. It was not until 1964 that I published Map of Another Town. *It was done by Little, Brown & Company and was dedicated to my cousin Nan Newton, who by mere chance was one of the dearest friends of my life.*

After I divorced Donald Friede in 1949 or perhaps 1950, I found that the only way I could earn a living for myself and my two girls was to write for magazines, and thanks to the guidance and patience of Henry Volkening I gradually built up a good name with several reputable periodicals. For many years it took all of my time and extra energy to cope with this new phase of my life, and I continued it for a long time, since all I needed was a pencil and paper, no matter where I might be sitting.

For a while, we lived at our Whittier ranch, where I had been a child, and I worked at the News *again as general handywoman for my father, and Anne and Mary went to schools there. Mother had died a few years before, and it was a godsend to my girls and me to find ourselves living with a fine old man, and of course it was good for him too: he loved us as much as we did him.*

After Rex died, we moved to Northern California, with his full blessing. At first he had been disappointed to learn of my decision to sell the paper after he died. It would have been a cinch, as he himself assured me, to stay on as editor in the town where he'd been a respected citizen for some forty-two years. What he did not realize was that what had been a little town of less than five thousand people when he moved there in 1911 was now a sprawling suburb of Los Angeles with several hundred thousand people calling it their headquarters. I felt no real emotional ties to it, and I was determined not to let my children breathe any more polluted air than they'd already absorbed. So we had the ranch house bulldozed to the ground; now a wading pool is there for other children, in a little park that Rex left in perpetuity so that the old men of the suburbs would have a place to meet and youngsters would have a place to play. And we pulled up stakes completely and settled in St. Helena, with never a moment's regret.

The next few years were very good ones emotionally and even physically. I could indeed earn enough for us to live on wherever we were, so that we spent about five years in Provence and Switzerland during the next decade. We were mostly in Aix, but for one year we lived in Lugano, and Anne and Mary learned to handle themselves more than commendably in Italian as well as French. Life was really fine, divided between the little California town that was immediately home to us, and the older places in a much older world.

After we came home from Aix-en-Provence the first time, in about 1955, I began to have very vivid dreams of the first French town I'd ever lived in, Dijon in Burgundy, and suddenly I was drawing, from those dreams, the map of still another town. Later but no less vivid in my conscious and subconscious worlds, this second map of Aix-en-Provence went very easily, and I like to feel that it is straight reporting of the fine life I lived there. The job was uncomplicated, and only my private life was somewhat less so, because Monique was living with us then, in St. Helena.

Monique's mother was a charming Frenchwoman, a new widow of a French engineer, trying to maintain an upper–middle class French household for her own four children in the old part of the Archbishop's palace, next to the cloister of the cathedral of St. Bénigne. On the recommendation of friends in Aix, my little girls lived with her for several months in this strange and beautiful place, and I saw them once or twice a week. (It was good practice for me in being lonely and has often stood me in fine stead.) While there were bad moments for Anne and Mary too, Monique's mother and the other children were robust good people, and my little girls fell very much in love with them all, in the impersonal way that only children really know. It seemed quite natural to them to assume that when we returned home, whenever that might be, Monique would come along. And to her mother's and my shared amazement and perhaps chagrin, this was exactly what happened.

Of course, by the time another year or so had passed in Aix, and the three young girls and I returned to St. Helena, Monique was sixteen and Anne was creeping up on her, and Kennedy was still half-unquestioning child and half-puzzled adolescent. Our resultant life was probably harder on me than on the three younger females, and after about a year and a half, it felt fine to head Monique toward New York–Marseille–Aix! I know, though, that we all learned a great deal about how to cope with our inner worlds, thanks to the presence of a fourth person in our small and possibly rather ingrown actuality.

And it seems impossible that deliberately as well as in our hearts, neither Monique nor the three of us have ever met again. I've never asked my girls if they wanted to see her, so truly loved during an important part of their lives.

When we went back to Aix, in 1958 or so, she was training to be a nurse in London. Now and then I hear a rumor; the last one was that a strange little old French lady in Marin County would reminisce compulsively to any audience about her years as governess to the two infant children of a well-known writer named Fisher. I refuse to believe this, of course, partly because Monique, when we knew her, was a tall thin adolescent and could not possibly have turned so quickly into an elderly French governess. What is more, she was never a governess in any way . . . any more than I was a famous writer. (Ho hum!)

I'll always remember two things about Monique, among a thousand other good ones, that really touched me: One time just before she left, she said with surprising sentimentality that there were indeed some things she would miss when she returned to Aix. I felt surprised at this unusual show of emotion in her somewhat surly attitude toward American life in general, and I wondered if perhaps she would finally admit that she would always think of Mary as a dear loving little friend. I asked her then, with some surety of her saying just this, what she would miss, and she replied without blinking that the thing she would most miss in this whole period of so many long months of good work and some good play too, was paper towels!

The other thing was that after we all had had a good little spree in San Francisco, my sister Anne took Monique down to the airport while I stayed in the hotel with the children. Mary turned very pale and listless, and went early to bed, while Anne and I watched the lights over the East Bay from our tall windows. Nothing more was said for several weeks about Monique's leaving or even about her having been with us for so long, but when we packed up the next morning to go back to St. Helena, I found a note under Mary's pillow. It said: "Tonight is a sad one. All I can hear is my heart. It is saying Monique . . . Monique . . Monique." I've always wished that I could feel as empty as that young girl did, at the departure of a friend, real or wishful.

In 1961, A Cordiall Water: A Garland of Odd & Old Receipts to Assuage the Ills of Man & Beast *was published by Little, Brown & Company. I wrote it while my girls and I were in Aix the second time, and I still find it a nice little book, written peacefully and in a true straightforward way. It is a tiny treatise about healing things like warts and nosebleeds and other minor tempests in our well-being, and much later when the editors of North Point Press asked me what I would like reprinted, I said without any hesitation that* A Cordiall Water *would be my choice.*

I was not sure, of course, that anybody would like it but me, because it had been a near-miss, the first time around, both here and in England. I said to the editor, perhaps rather feebly, that I thought the book was therapeutic, and might sell well in airports, to reassure or otherwise comfort troubled travelers. Sure enough, a batch taken to the San Francisco airport was bought immediately by about fifty unknown passengers, and I like to think that it helped them reach their destinations, if nothing more. I still feel fine about its new life, which continues lustily, and am pleased that I could write at least one book that I can recommend, no matter how sheepishly.

In 1968 I published with G. P. Putnam's Sons a book of essays and articles that had already appeared in the New Yorker. *We called it* With Bold Knife and Fork. *It had the shortest introduction I've ever written, probably, and it was dedicated to my grandmother Mary Frances Oliver Holbrook. I wrote it for money, and it was an enjoyable job.*

I had originally intended to do a short thing for my friend William Targ, who was then senior editor at Putnam's, about recipes that were simply too horrible to be repeated in anything except a half-ridiculous kind of spoof. But when I started to go through my file for the real monstrosities in it, I found that there were too many decent recipes to ignore. Most of them were family hand-me-downs, the Tried-and-Trues . . . things like Cousin Aggie's Spanish Bun and other relics from the plain days in American cooking, attributed to friends or cooks, or even close relatives. To my surprise the book was accepted enthusiastically by the finicky magazine staff, and Mr. Shawn himself is reported to have said, "Dang blast it!"—or whatever expletive such a godlike figure might use—"The woman can make even tripe *sound edible." This was praise from Heaven itself, and so received.*

I admit to having read parts of the first chapter of With Bold Knife. *And I feel quite proud of "The Anatomy of a Recipe." It is often used by reputable chefs and cooking school professors as an example of the only correct procedure for either writing or following one. The method is infallible, and I say this without any mock humility whatsoever, since it is not* mine.

Every January, when the navel oranges are at their best, I look up the recipe in Bold Knife *for Edith's Orange Marmalade. I spent a great deal of time honing the language in that short paragraph, to make the method impeccable to even the worst fools among us. And still, I am often annoyed as all hell to have a good cook tell me smugly that the jam did not jell, or otherwise do what it was supposed to. Invariably, I find that my meticulous directions were not* followed. *Ho hum.*

And there are other things in the book that are almost as good as the marmalade and the first small masterpiece of Chapter One. In other words, I seem to be rather satisfied with the job! I suppose that eventually it will be reprinted, but so far sales continue to be good enough to justify Putnam's hanging on to it.

My next book, about growing up in the Quaker community of Whittier, California, was a very far cry from the deliberate commercialism I practiced in With Bold Knife and Fork. *It was named* Among Friends *by Judith Jones of Knopf, and I was so pleased to find myself at last in the almost-holy confines of this publishing house that I'd wished to join ever since I first wrote* Serve It Forth *and got a fan letter from Alfred Knopf himself, that I did not care one way or the other that the title was a kind of pun. By nature I do not like puns, except when they happen in conversation. Certainly I cannot agree with my mother's far from original verdict that a pun is the lowest form of wit. I simply do not like them in titles, no matter how apt they may be.*

I wrote Among Friends *in Bridgehampton and Sag Harbor, and it was probably the hardest work I'd ever done. I was completely alone for one winter, except for three dates for dinner and lunch, and two walks in the woods with a passing friend. I sweated like a stevedore, literally, over the actual turmoil that I'd made for myself, because I was determined to prove that most of us do not remember the real facts of something from our childhood, but instead recall what we were told we remembered by our parents and teachers.*

It was hard as Hell itself to strip down all the wishful dreams of what had really happened with Cousin Lizzy Beatty, for instance. She stayed with us before she became completely batty, on her return from some fifty years in China as doctor to the Dowager Empress. She spoke mostly in Chinese, and I spent more time with her than anyone else in the family, simply because we understood each other. She told me long stories, which I later repeated to my sister in English, but how was this? When I first heard them in her upper-class singsong from another world, another culture, who was understanding whom?

And then there were the things I remembered about school: what had really happened the day my young Quaker friends taunted me about being in love with Red Sutherland, so that finally I flung a daring kiss toward his back some twenty yards ahead of me, and then turned on my tormentors and laughed and stuck out my tongue at them? All this sounds very silly by now, but in Sag Harbor I had to straighten it out and reduce it to its basic action, strip it of all the prettiness and perhaps the gentility that Time had lent. I did not want to remember what I was told to. I had to get past all that wishful guff I'd been fed. I wanted to go as far back as possible in my own recollections of many things that were still telling to me that I had been an isolated child, teased and tormented and twisted by prejudices that were beyond my recognition then, but that I was safe and happy always, because I was loved and trusted.

I learned very early that my little Quaker friends had not teased me because they hated me, but because they had been taught by their parents, more often than not unwittingly, to dislike and mock people who did not believe as they did.

Many years later, the same thing happened to my own older daughter, when very soon after she learned enough French in Aix-en-Provence to understand her friends, she asked me seriously one night how she smelled. I said that to me she smelled fine, although perhaps a little more so than in America because we took fewer baths in the sixteenth-century houses than we did in the newer culture of California. She asked, "But do I smell like an American? What does an American really smell like?" And I found that one of her schoolmates had come into the room and taken one cold look at Anne and said, "I can't stay here. I smell Yankees somewhere . . ."

So I told my nine-year-old girl about the obvious reasons for this. The parents of the young French girl had helped her survive Occupation, Liberation, all the nightmares of having strangers everywhere. They came to hate "other" people— the way Quakers had not liked the "others" in Whittier—even if they had been asked to come, temporarily, *as my own father had been . . . as the Brits and Yankees had been, in France. The helpless Aixois, just like the helpless "Friends" of my own childhood, had made us "different." Of* course *we smelled, because we were the outsiders. And now my little girl must be aware of this, and as acceptant of it as I had once learned to be.*

I am glad I wrote the book. It cleaned my own inner air, but it is not as forceful as I wanted it to be, and I feel unhappy that it offended some of the people in Whittier, because that is something that I would never want to do. It is of small comfort to me that the severest critics among them admit that they have never read the book itself. It seems that while I was comfortably back in France again, this time with my sister Norah, a national broadcast said that I had written that all Quakers were bastards. This of course was impossible, but I never had a chance to refute the reviewer's taking out of context a few such damning words. What I had written was something like, "Some Quakers are saints and some are bastards" . . . And the damage was done, and there is no way to change any such savored prejudice except to realize more strongly than ever that even among Friends one is not completely free from small prejudices, and from tiny lapses in brotherly love.

I wrote my next book, published by Knopf in 1978, during and after a stay of several months in Marseille with Norah Barr. I called it A Considerable Town, *and the endpapers and its handsome binding were taken from an old map I found there, and not from the ones inside my head for both Aix and Dijon.*

Norah and I had a beautiful little flat out toward the mouth of the Old Port, just above the almost deserted barracks, and then the dry docks of the Foreign Legion. It was a magical experience, and like almost every one in my life, I'd gladly relive it.

The book about it is not at all like the one it has been linked with, by the publishers, that I wrote so many years before about Aix. Some people in Marseille were scornful and disbelieving that anybody could presume to know enough about their town to put it into print, or they suspected that I was foolhardy to tackle such an indescribably evil and mysterious town as they blandly and perhaps rightly assume Marseille to be. Maybe they are right. But I think in the last chapter of the book, which I called "A Conclusion," rather than an afterword, I made my reasons clear. I dedicated the book to my two girls and my sister Norah, because they, like me, are part Marseillaises.

The book called As They Were, *which Knopf brought out in 1982, was the result of a suggestion made by somebody at Knopf. The idea was that I would collect a whole lot of things from other books and magazines and my own un-printed materials, to make something I myself would have called "Other Places." It was to be the third of a trilogy with the two books about Aix and Marseille. For some reason, this plan was dropped, and* As They Were *was published without any reference in its publicity to either of the other books. (They in turn were*

published together by the Vintage paperback section of Knopf, and called Two
Towns in Provence.)

As They Were *does not much interest me, although it sold well, I was in-
formed. The only thing I really remember about it is that an English friend wrote
to me in a rather scoffing way about the title, saying that in our American lingo
it should more properly be* Like They Was. *I was not too amused by this, of
course. (This book I dedicated to my sister Norah, again.)*

Sister Age *was put together in 1983 and is a collection of stories that I had
published or written over the past three decades. I did a serious foreword and
afterword for it, because I admit to being impressed by how long I had been thinking and in fact chewing over the subject of aging.*

*Nobody was much interested in publishing this book, although Alfred Knopf
and Judith Jones apparently were willing to risk a flop. The general feeling had
been for many years that it was a waste of time to bother to write anything about
a subject that was dimly viewed when it was not deliberately ignored. Everyone
was sure that old people hated to read about themselves and that young people
were bored by their elders.*

*Of course, I have never agreed with either of these views, and the fact that the
book has sold well perhaps proves that I was right. It is heartwarming to me to
hear from people of every age about something I've written in this book. It gives
me a general feeling of real enjoyment, and a kind of excitement, to find that so
many other people want to learn and think about something that is too often closed
out of our usual conscious patterns.*

*The foreword and afterword talk about an old painting on leather I have kept
for many years. It is the picture of an old woman called Ursula von Ott, painted
by her son in 1808, and it was an expression of all his traditionally adolescent
loathing of his mother, whom he plainly felt was socially and aesthetically inferior
to him.*

*The oddest thing about this picture, though, and the one that first drew me to
it many years ago, was the remote look of amusement on her monkeylike old face.
There she stood, and there she still stands, alone, remote. This was astonishing to
me, and I still don't understand it, and that is why I wrote her book, and called
it and her my sister, Age.*

serve it *forth*

To Begin

"Of course," concluded Robert Kilburn Root, sitting cross-legged and contemplating his shashlik, "of course if this book is well larded with anecdotes, it will of necessity be short."

There are two kinds of books about eating: those that try to imitate Brillat-Savarin's, and those that try not to. The first substitute whimsy for his wit, and dull reminiscences for his delightful anecdotes. The second are gross where he would be delicate, and choose blunt statistics rather than his piercing observations.

And books about what to eat: they too are twins from one source, the first written recipes in our world. They are stodgy, matter-of-fact, covered very practically with washable cloth or gravy-colored paper, beginning with measurements and food values and ending with sections on the care of invalids—oddly enough for books so concerned with hygiene! They are usually German or English or American.

Or, on the other hand, they are short, bound impractically in creamy paper or chintz, illustrated by woodcutters *à la mode*. They begin with witty philosophizing on the pleasures of the table, and end with a suggested menu for an intimate dinner given to seven gentlemen who know his wife, by a wealthy old banker who feels horns pricking up gently from his bald skull. These books are usually French. They are much more entertaining, if less useful, than their phlegmatic twins.

To make one into two yet again, there are two painful variants of one most interesting subject: those who eat. The first, foisted upon us at least semiannually by enthusiastic publishers, is listed under *Memoirs* in book catalogues. Its pages totter and crumple under a weight of well-known names, and from each chapter rises a reek, a heady stench of truffles, Château Yquem, and quails *financière*. You sit, pompously nonchalant, on a balcony at Monte Carlo, *tête-à-tête* with three princes, a millionaire, and the lovely toast of London, God bless her! Or, in a Georgian dining room filled with quietly munching Cabinet ministers, you exchange quips that grow by repetition into *fin de siècle* epigrams. It is all very enervating—and it sells well, they say.

Its partner, that other kind of book about people who eat, is at times even more objectionable. It is usually written by two self-styled gourmets, or three. It shows pictures of its authors standing beside a quaint old inn near Oxford or a quaint old inn near Cannes. It discusses seriously and with firm authority the problem of Bordeaux versus Burgundies or when to drink Barsac, and settles with a fine confidence all questions of vintage, pourboires, and the barbaric horrors of the cocktail. It is perhaps needless to say that its authors are young and full of intellectual fun and frolic, and that they are making a gastronomic tour on bicycles.

Now I am going to write a book. It will be about eating and about what to eat and about people who eat. And I shall do gymnastics by trying to fall between these three fires, or by straddling them all.

The first, that great ghost born in Belley who ate like a fat parson and wrote consummately on eating with delicate art, I shall very humbly recognize.

The second—was it a Sicilian cooking for Cæsar or a Norman chef in old England who first wrote our plans for dishes, or was it perhaps a round monk in Touraine?—the second I shall avoid. Recipes in my book will be there like birds in a tree—if there is a comfortable branch.

The third I can most easily miss. I am not old and famous, with friends whose names sound like the guest-lists of all the diplomatic receptions held in all the world capitals since 1872. Nor am I young and intellectually gastronomic on a bicycle.

So my book, hopefully evading each of the three fires, will be singed by all. Brillat-Savarin will haunt it, and very probably show himself in an inevitable aphorism. *The Settlement Cookbook* and Paul Reboux will peer shyly and with little recognition at their ancestors *The Harleian Manuscript* and Mrs. Glasse and Carême and Roselli. And people I know will talk a little and eat more, not with prime ministers in Geneva, perhaps, nor with munitions-makers at Menton. But they are really very nice people, most of them.

I serve it forth.

To End

We lived, once, above a little pastry shop that called itself "At the Sign of the Fin Gourmet." It sold probably the worst apricot tarts that ever sogged and stuck in throat.

"*N'est pas gourmand qui veut,*" said Brillat-Savarin. The aphorism is, as I predicted at the first, inevitable. Truly a man is not a gourmand, much less a *fin gourmet*, by wishing to be so.

1942

How to cook a wolf

Introduction to the Revised Edition (1951)

It is hard to know whether war or peace makes the greater changes in our vocabularies, both of the tongue and of the spirit.

Certain it is, however, that in less than ten years this book about living as decently as possible with the ration cards and blackouts and like miseries of World War II has assumed some of the characteristics of quaintness. It has become, in short, in so short a time, a kind of period piece. In its own way it is as curious, as odd, as any fat old gold-ribbed volume called, a hundred years ago instead of nine or ten, *Ladies' Indispensable Assistant and Companion, One of the Best Systems of Cookery Ever Published for Sister, Mother, and Wife*. . . .

Of course, it is difficult, in spite of the obvious changes in our physical problems since *How to Cook a Wolf* was first published in 1942, to say truthfully and exactly when we are at war.

Now we are free of ration cards (It was shocking, the other day, to hear that after almost twelve years gas rationing had come to an end in England.

What a long time! Too long . . .): no more blue and red tokens, no more flimsy stamps to tear out or not tear out.

We can buy as much porterhouse and bourbon and powdered sugar as our purses will allow, given the rise of almost 100 percent in the cost of such gastronomical amenities.

We need not worry, temporarily at least, about basic cupboards for blackouts . . . while at the same time we try not to think, even superficially, about what and when and how and where to nourish survivors of the next kind of bomb.

Thus stated, the case for Peace is feeble.

One less chilling aspect of the case for World War II is that while it was still a shooting affair it taught us survivors a great deal about daily living which is valuable to us now that it is, ethically at least, a question of cold weapons and hot words. (In one week from the writing of this cautious statement, or one hour from the final printing of it, double ridicule can be its lot. Are weapons ever cold?)

There are very few men and women, I suspect, who cooked and marketed their way through the past war without losing forever some of the nonchalant extravagance of the Twenties. They will feel, until their final days on earth, a kind of culinary caution: butter, no matter how unlimited, is a precious substance not lightly to be wasted; meats, too, and eggs, and all the far-brought spices of the world, take on a new significance, having once been so rare. And that is good, for there can be no more shameful carelessness than with the food we eat for life itself. When we exist without thought or thanksgiving we are not men, but beasts.

War is a beastly business, it is true, but one proof that we are human is our ability to learn, even from it, how better to exist. If this book, written in one wartime, still goes on helping to solve that unavoidable problem, it is worth reading again, I think, no matter what its quaint superficiality, its sometimes unintentionally grim humor.

That is why I have added to it, copiously. Not everything new in it is purely practical, of course. But even the wolf, temporarily appeased, cannot live on bread alone.

And *that* is why I have added even more, and may have sneaked other recipes into the book. Some are hopelessly extravagant (16 eggs!) and some are useful and some are funny, and one is actually for bread that even a wolf would live on.

These "extra" recipes are culinary rules to be followed with not a thought of the budget, nor even half an ear cocked toward that sniffing at the door. I know, because I *know*, that one good whiff from any of these dishes will send the beast cringing away, in a kind of extrasensory and ultra-moral embarrassment.

1943

The Gastronomical Me

FOREWORD

People ask me: Why do you write about food, and eating and drinking?
Why don't you write about the struggle for power and security, and about
love, the way the others do?

They ask it accusingly, as if I were somehow gross, unfaithful to the
honor of my craft.

The easiest answer is to say that, like most other humans, I am hungry.
But there is more than that. It seems to me that our three basic needs, for
food and security and love, are so mixed and mingled and entwined that we
cannot straightly think of one without the others. So it happens that when
I write of hunger, I am really writing about love and the hunger for it, and
warmth and the love of it and the hunger for it . . . and then the warmth
and richness and fine reality of hunger satisfied . . . and it is all one.

I tell about myself, and how I ate bread on a lasting hillside, or drank red
wine in a room now blown to bits, and it happens without my willing it that

I am telling too about the people with me then, and their other deeper needs for love and happiness.

There is food in the bowl, and more often than not, because of what honesty I have, there is nourishment in the heart, to feed the wilder, more insistent hungers. We must eat. If, in the face of that dread fact, we can find other nourishment, and tolerance and compassion for it, we'll be no less full of human dignity.

There is a communion of more than our bodies when bread is broken and wine drunk. And that is my answer, when people ask me: Why do you write about hunger, and not wars or love?

1946

Here Let Us Feast

A BOOK OF BANQUETS

THE BOOK AND THE FLEA

That's a valiant flea that dare eat his breakfast on the lip of a lion.
—Shakespeare,King Henry V

This book is about feasting. It is a collection of excerpts—sentences, and paragraphs, and even pages—all of them concerned with man's fundamental need to celebrate the high points of his life by eating and drinking. It is true that such a subject is not always connected, perforce, with the fine art of gastronomy, but still it is honest and intrinsically necessary in any human scheme, any plan for the future, any racial memory. And I feel that, like a familiar speaker at a banquet, it "needs no introduction." Feasting is part of life itself, and has been since cavemen first celebrated victory by gorging on half-raw meat, in peace and safety after their battles.

Men have always feasted, in huts and palaces and temples, in an instinctive gesture of gratitude to their gods for the good things that have come to them, and it is symbolical of their basic trust and artlessness that bread and wine, the good things themselves, are what they offer back. It is their way of admitting, subconsciously or not, that hunger is more than a problem of belly and guts, and that the satisfying of it can and must and does nourish the spirit as well as the body.

Food for the soul is a part of all religion, as African savages know when they roast a tiger's heart for their god, as Christians know when they reverently partake of Body and Blood at the mystical feast of Holy Communion.

That is why there can be an equal significance in a sumptuous banquet for five thousand heroes, with the king sitting on his iron throne and minstrels singing above the sound of gnawed bones and clinking cups, or in a piece of dry bread eaten alone by a man lifting his eyes unto the hills.

That is why, to my mind, there can be nothing irreverent or illogical about putting together in one collection of feasts such apparently disparate things as St. Luke's story of the Last Supper and Lewis Carroll's tea-party for Alice in Wonderland, the fish fry for the Lord God in His green pastures and Trimalchio's gluttonous orgy in decadent Rome.

There is, of course, one obvious danger to any such arbitrary choosing, and I am aware of it but not afraid: I know that anyone who reads this book may wonder why in the name of intelligence and taste and even common sense I have chosen as I have. Why have I left out Falstaff, and Sancho Panza, and Chaucer's gourmande nun? How have I dared print Maginn's *Story Without a Tail* and ignore Thomas Love Peacock's erudite and slyly ribald drinking songs? The answer is only that this is part of what I have read and remembered as good, in some thirty years. In thirty more the whole thing would be different, the choice a wider one . . . if not narrower!

I have always found gastronomy a fulfilling subject, and have read much about it without surfeit. I know just what anyone knows who has read the books I have read, with anything like my own keen if unscholarly interest: that is, I have a sketchy but personally entertaining fund of common knowledge, some of it faulty, much of it garbled by time and my own interpretations of it, all of it alive for me . . . not sleeping in my brain.

There are several authoritative and even interesting books, full of dates and such, which are much safer than this one could possibly be for a reader who wants to know the chemical formula for manna, when and how Solomon feasted the Queen of Sheba, what Elizabeth of England spent in one year on her breakfast ale. And there are lists telling just what are the gastronomical classics . . . lists which almost certainly will never include *The Peterkin Papers*, or *Jorrock's Jaunts and Jollities*, but will lend much more weight than this book's index to anyone's need to be a well-read gastronome.

I have read the lists, and the books, and I still have the temerity, not bland or smug but quite conscious of its implications, to make this present collection public.

I am a valiant flea indeed, thus to dare perch upon the lip of such a lion as the literature of feasting! My breakfast has been good. I shall hop back, again and again, to feed my little body and my growing soul upon such inexhaustible nourishment.

The End

We are alive indeed, fed by the countless feasts of other men, other times. As long as we breathe we can thus nourish ourselves, valiant fleas upon the lion's lip, sucking richness and strength from what has always been written, and always will be, about the manners and the meanings of broken bread, poured wine, and the communion of two or three of us gathered together. . . .

1947

Not Now But NOW

AFTERWORD

The reason I wrote this book is that two men I dearly loved told me to. One said, "You can do it, and you should." The other said, "You must." So I did, to please them.

Pascal Covici, who ended his long life as one of the last of the "true breed" of editors, started it in Chicago as part-owner of one of those mysteriously potent bookstores that happen in places like Paris and Budapest, and even in Los Angeles when someone like Jake Zeitlin is there . . . or in any smaller town where eager impatient minds must seek out good talk. In Covici's correctly shabby, dusty rendezvous, stripling giants like Theodore Dreiser and Ben Hecht decided the future of the world. Then Pat moved on to New York, to be half of what soon became a prestigious publishing firm, Covici-Friede.

Donald Friede was a well-heeled international roamer in search of cultural reassurance. At one point in his adolescence his mother sent him to a psychiatric–vocational counselor. The famous doctor, after long talks with

Donald, who said later that they were mostly about why *Nicholas Nickleby* was his favorite book, told her that the boy should become either an art dealer or a publisher. So at twenty-one, after going to Harvard, Princeton, and Yale in one year, he was installed as a vice president in the Horace Liveright kingdom, where he tried hard for a while to be useful about emptying wastebaskets. (He once said mildly, "It is very hard to be a rich Jewish boy. It is harder to be a rich Jewish office boy. But it is perhaps hardest to be a fat rich Jewish office boy.")

In a few years Covici-Friede published a lot of high-class prizewinners and some flops. Then the two parted, thanks perhaps to the current Depression, but with genuine respect and affection. Covici went on to be editor at Viking and Friede paced restlessly through the Western cultural scene, in Paris and Hollywood and New York.

Both men were attractive and exciting, with varying but always good tastes in books, words, typography, women, paintings, wines. For a time Donald and I were married and Pat was my editor. Both stayed my friends: in Pat's case my mentor and in Donald's the guardian angel of our two daughters. And somewhere they told me, *told me*, to write a novel.

I said, "But I am not a novelist. Some people are and some . . . I've been reading novels all my life, and I don't want to try to write one." Obviously I had little chance to escape their professional and financial pressures, no matter how subtly or bluntly applied, so I sat down and wrote *Not Now but Now*. It was something I "could and should and must do . . ."

I decided to make up the whole thing and tell it through a person as totally as possible unlike myself, both physically and morally. I knew I could tell dreams and spin yarns, although always I must depend on some of my own experience. I did finish the book and send it on to a delighted Pat, while Donald congratulated me on a "perfect vehicle" for some movie star he was then promoting.

The "novel" got good reviews, but was a commercial turnip. Pat kept on being my gentle editor, but Donald gave up any dreams of my ever writing a best-seller.

As for the book itself, I was never interested in it, once done, and still feel that North Point Press may be zany to reprint it. But perhaps it was written, no matter how doggedly, a little ahead of its time. To my mind it is really not a novel at all, although Covici was determined to call it that. It is a string of short stories, tied together more or less artfully by a time-trick. The female Jennie appears everywhere, often with heedless cruelty or deliberate destruction to her docile associates, and then slips away in her little snakeskin shoes . . .

Of course I had to borrow from my own life, since I do not often remember any other, so that it was I who met the undertaker from Lausanne, and so on. The conservation of energy is almost as grave a problem as the Eternal Bitch and the liberation of women, whatever they all may be.

So I'd been told to write a novel and I did my honest best. I still love the two autocratic rascals who thus commanded me, and I hope the present publishers are justified in their stubborn belief that this is indeed a *book*, anyway. All I can do is keep on trying to write a good and pleasing sentence, even if nobody tells me to.

1949

The Physiology of Taste

OR, MEDITATIONS ON
TRANSCENDENTAL GASTRONOMY
by JEAN ANTHELME BRILLAT-SAVARIN

THE TRANSLATOR'S PREFACE

I made this translation by myself, and can therefore thank none for it but perhaps my first schoolteacher, who showed me how to read. I have put it into the simplest words I know, since I feel that it is a singularly straight-forward and unornamented piece of prose to have been written in a flowery literary period. I have kept as far as possible its measured rhythm, and have changed into colons only a few overburdened commas and semicolons. As I have more than once pointed out along the way, the Professor's idiosyncrasies of spelling foreign words I have accentuated with SPACED SMALL CAPS LIKE THESE, to differentiate them from his own stressed words. I emerge from the real ordeal of translation with an even realer humility.

As for the numerous glosses that I have thus humbly added to the text, I can give thanks, but not enough, to several friends who have helped me. Lawrence Clark Powell and Robert Vosper of the Library of the University of California at Los Angeles let me call upon them for anything I wanted from their prodigious stacks, and H. Richard Archer of the William Andrews Clark Memorial Library in Los Angeles did the same from his more limited and perhaps more precious shelves. The three of them added hours of their own and their staffs' time to track down abstruse, possibly unimportant, but interesting notes for me. Miss Althea Warren, then head of the Los Angeles Public Libraries, and one of her witty and seemingly tireless assistants named Armine Mackenzie, were unreasonably generous of their time and advice. I could use the rare and often fantastic gastronomical library of Harold H. Price of San Francisco. I could call on the energetic and profound knowledge of Dr. Henry B. Bieler of Pasadena, for not only biological but spiritual data connected with the miracle of hunger and its perils and pleasures. I could depend upon the conscience of Frances Wolf to plunge dauntlessly into batch after batch of finicky transcribing of my two-finger type. In countless moments of despair, chagrin, exasperation (but never boredom), I could turn to the ruthless editorial eye of Donald Friede.

For all this I hold myself blessed among translators, and I will end my honest labor with the hope that what I have done will find more favor than blame among the four (and more) categories of gastronomers that Brillat-Savarin wrote of in 1825. It has taken me only some two years to translate what he spent perhaps twenty-five or thirty years writing.

That is as it should be.

A Postscript from the Translator

I feel even more strongly than I did at the beginning of translating this book that it is a well-balanced expression of one thinking man's attitude toward life. There are few of them, in any language.

The fact that *The Physiology of Taste* is about gastronomy has little, nothing really, to do with its author's innate good taste, nor with his art in making it clear upon each page. I have plumbed every word of his, and after many years of casual enjoyment and two of the most intimate kind, I have yet to find myself either bored or offended, which is more than most women can say of any relationship, whether ghostly or corporeal. For me, the Professor is a continuing delight.

I enjoy the physical picture of him, which may be wishful but is still based on a few descriptions beside his own, and a few engravings, and a few phrases like Charles Monselet's: "This figure, smiling rather than laughing, this well-lined paunch, this stylish mind and stomach . . ."

I enjoy his "stylish mind" most of all: his teasing of the priests, and his underplayed pleasure in them when they were good men of any cloth; his tenderness and irony toward pretty women, and his full fine enjoyment of them; his lusty delight in hunting, in a good row, in a cock-snoot at disaster . . . and the way he made all this plain to me, in a prose perhaps more straightforward than any that has come down to us from his verbose flighty period in French literature.

His restrained discretion, while never simpering or ridiculous, is often deliberately pedagogic. He sometimes harrumphs, tongue in cheek . . . no insignificant feat either physically or spiritually! He often plays, tongue still in cheek, the safely retired satyr . . . but never does he grow offensive or even faintly senile. Deliberately at times he outlines with mocking pedantry the A-B-C, a-b-c of a point. Never does he scorn the plodders of philosophy who have made banalities of such ways of logic. Always there is clear in everything he writes a basic humility, and that is the main reason why I think his book is one meant to last much longer than a century or so. That is why I have spent many months of my best thought and my best (my *vintage*) energy upon it.

In a Western world filled with too many books, too many human beings angry or bored enough to be voluble, it is a good thing that there are a few such distillations as this one. Brillat-Savarin spent about twenty-five years writing it. He spoke of it to almost nobody, and when finally it appeared, a few months before his death and anonymously and at his own expense, his friends were astounded that he had written it, for he had never flashed before them in its full colors the rich tapestry of his mind, but had instead woven quietly and in secret peace.

In the Professor's time it was considered the unquestioned right of any man of common sense, which he so eminently was, to choose how best he might spend his hours of creation. When young he studied war and love and politics with an ardor and directness and an unclouded simplicity impossible to our own murky days. When he grew older, and withdrew perforce from actual combat, he found himself in the happy state of being able to think, to recollect in tranquillity.

That is perhaps the greatest difference between him and us: by the time we have slugged our way as courageously as possible past the onslaughts of modern engines and bacteria and ideals we are drained and exhausted, and any one of us who reaches the age of seventy-one with serenity and a clear conscience is felt to be an unfair freak. Something must be wrong, we say resentfully; he must have cheated somewhere, taken some secret elixir . . .

Perhaps we can sip that potion, even vicariously, in the slow reading of a few books like this one, and can feel ourselves encouraged and renewed by the knowledge that if Brillat-Savarin could outride the wild storms of revolution and intrigue and not let them trouble his digestion, as Balzac wrote of him, so in our way can we.

An Alphabet for Gourmets

A Foreword

It is apparently impossible for me to say anything about gastronomy, the art and science of satisfying one of our three basic human needs, without involving myself in what might be called side issues—might be, that is, by anyone who does not believe, as I do, that it is futile to consider hunger as a thing separate from people who are hungry.

That is why, when I set myself to follow anything as seemingly arbitrary as an alphabet, with its honored and unchanging sequence and its firm count of twenty-six letters, I must keep myself well in hand lest I find *A Is for Apple, B Is for Borscht*, and *C Is for Codfish Cakes* turning into one novel, one political diatribe, and one nonfiction book on the strange lovemakings of sea monsters, each written largely in terms of eating, drinking, digesting, and each written by *me*, shaped, molded, and, to some minds, distorted by my own vision, which depends in turn on my state of health, passion, finances, and my general glandular balance.

If a woman can be made more peaceful, a man fuller and richer, children happier, by a changed approach to the basically brutish satisfaction of hunger, why should not I, the person who brought about that change, feel a definite and rewarding urge to proselytize? If a young man can learn to woo with cup and spoon as well as with his inborn virility, why should not I, who showed him how, feel myself among Gasterea's anointed? The possibilities for bettering the somewhat dingy patterns of life on earth by a new interest in how best to stay our human hunger are so infinite that, to my mind at least, some such tyrannical limitations as an ABC will impose are almost requisite.

The alphabet is also controversial, which in itself is good. Why, someone may ask, did I scamp such lush fields as *L Is for Lucullus, G Is for Gourmet*? Why did I end the alphabet with a discussion of the hors d'oeuvres called *zakuski*, surely more appropriate at the beginning of any feast, literary or otherwise, and ignore the fine fancies to be evoked by the word zabaglione, with all its connotations of sweet satisfaction and high flavor?

I do not really know, but most probably because I am myself. This ABC is the way *I* wrote it. There is room between its lines, and even its words, for each man to write his own gastronomical beliefs, call forth his own remembered feastings, and taste once more upon his mind's tongue the wine and the clear rock-water of cups uncountable.

A *Cordiall* *water*

A GARLAND OF ODD & OLD RECEIPTS TO ASSUAGE THE ILLS OF MAN & BEAST

PREFACE

Sometimes people ask me what I think is the best book I have written. My only answer is that I have never been satisfied. But, as things now stand, I feel that my translation of Brillat-Savarin's *Physiology of Taste* (which of course I did not *write*) and *A Cordiall Water* are perhaps the pick of the litter.

The reason I like this little book about folk medicine is that its prose seems to have a purity about it that I have long sensed in writers who are thinking in two languages. I never tried to attain this. Joseph Conrad had it, and so did Nabokov and other greater workers than I could ever be. But for a few hours, while I was writing about horny cats and aching bones and nosebleeds, and all that clutter of life, I was stripped of banality, and I wrote simply in my native tongue, because I was temporarily detached from it and thus more aware.

In about 1960 my two daughters and I were living into our fourth year in Aix-en-Provence. They left for their classes before eight, and came back after six at night. They worked hard, and so did I. We had two rooms on the fifth floor of the old Hôtel de Provence, and we met for lunch on the cours Mirabeau and sat for a couple of hours, eating lightly. At night, because the hotel had no restaurant, we scrounged happily around town.

So while my girls dug into Racine and Giono I tidied some mental drawers about folk medicine, and what I wrote in the quiet room above the rooftops of the old town came out as this little book. I believe that it has a pleasant honesty of style, and I hope I am not mistaken.

CONCLUSION

Men freely believe that which they desire.
—*Shakespeare*, Julius Caesar

And here are two recipes, perhaps to prove this book's possible excuse.

For a Consumpsion
Take 30 garden snails & 30 Earth worms of middling sise, bruise ye snails & wash them & ye worms in fair waters, cut ye worms in peices. Boil these in a quart of Spring water to a pint. Pour it boiling on 2 ounses of Candied Eringo root sliced thin. When it is cold strain it thro a fine flannel bag. Take a quarter of a pint of it warm, with an Equal Quantity of Cows' milk till well, at twilight.

Truth . . . Faith . . . Miracles!
Come tonight to the Mission of Divine Healing, where the Deliverance of Man will be announced! There will be the Laying on of Hands!! Testimonies of Heavenly Cures will be Made Aloud!!! Come with Faith, and you will find Peace, Health, and Happiness! Free Admission!!!

The first receipt is from the journal kept by a London apothecary in Shakespeare's time. The second is from a handbill thrust at me once in France by a tall man dressed in rough, thick clothes.

It was night. Down the side street from which he darted now and then with his bunch of flimsy papers I could hear the quavering of a dismal hymn. It sounded strange in the dark, sung perhaps by five or six ancient women, and its Wesleyan measures were doubly foreign in that Catholic town where Campra had been born and where schoolboys whistled phrases from the Jerusalem Psalter as much as they did from the latest rock-and-roll. But the handbill was no stranger to me than the other recipe, for both spoke of incantation, and mystery, and ageless faith: the essentials of healing.

1964

Map of Another Town

A MEMOIR OF PROVENCE

...it is very probable that if I had to draw the portrait of Paris, I would, one more time, draw it of myself.
—Jean Giono, 1961

Often in the sketch for a portrait, the invisible lines that bridge one stroke of the pencil or brush to another are what really make it live. This is probably true in a word picture too. The myriad undrawn unwritten lines are the ones that hold together what the painter and the writer have tried to set down, their own visions of a thing: a town, one town, this town.

Not everything can be told, nor need it be, just as the artist himself need not and indeed cannot reveal every outline of his vision.

There before us is what one human being has seen of something many others have viewed differently, and the lines held back are perhaps the ones most vital to the whole.

Here before me now is my picture, my map, of a place and therefore of myself, and much that can never be said adds to its reality for me, just as much of its reality is based on my own shadows, my inventions.

Over the years I have taught myself, and have been taught, to be a stranger. A stranger usually has the normal five senses, perhaps especially so, ready to protect and nourish him.

Then there are the extra senses that function only in subconsciousness. These are perhaps a stranger's best allies, the ones that stay on and grow stronger as time passes and immediacy dwindles.

It is with the invisible ink distilled from all these senses, then, that I have drawn this map of a town, a place real in stone and water, and in the spirit, which may also be realer.

1969

with Bold Knife and Fork

INTRODUCTION

This book is about how I like to cook, most of the time, for people in my world, and it gives some of the reasons. These have made life enjoyable, so they may be of interest to other human beings.

Among Friends

PROLOGUE: CHILD OF AN INNER "GHETTO"

There is a kind of withdrawal, courteous but cabalistic, that a person meets in trying to talk with Quakers about their faith, if he is not a member of the Society of Friends and is plainly not trying to become one. At the opposite end of the pole of discipline and self-control there is the dewy-eyed sentimentality of people of other Christian sects who think of Quakers as men of infinite brotherhood and patience, and of understanding and goodwill and everything basically to be desired but left unattained in modern life, at least by non-Quakers. Between these two extremes, which are no more so than those between a Sephardic Jew from Lisbon and a band of hippie poets who have served their time in the Haight-Ashbury, there is the kind of Quakers I grew up with, when I was a child in Whittier, California.

All children can be cruel, and all children mimic their elders, and I was often teased, indirectly for being a non-Quaker and directly for being of foreign descent, by the peers who walked amiably every morning to school with me, sat with me all day without a sneer or snub, and then often turned vicious on the way home. The interesting thing about their almost ritual tauntings, which faded and flared according to the moon and the seasons, was that I knew nothing of cruelty as such, and thought theirs was part of normal life. My friends, for such they were, were only saying mocking things they had heard at home, from the kind quiet lips of their Quaker parents.

I do not remember hearing anything at all about *them* from my own father and mother, except an occasional and gentle quip made by the banker, Amos Maple, which my father would repeat at luncheon with relish. These witticisms were usually based on the sly use of an Old Testament quotation, and there was nothing but admiration in my sire's enjoyment of them. They were what was new on the Rialto that morning, at the intersection of Green-leaf and Philadelphia in the little town, and therefore they could be savored in the ghettos by anyone privileged enough to have caught them. My parents enjoyed the play of human wit as deeply as did the Quaker moneylender. Perhaps this intimate attitude of awareness, in my family, contributed to my early acceptance of my schoolmates' conditioned teasings; perhaps my bland immunity was as cruel as theirs.

My father, Rex Kennedy, was an intruder in the predominantly Quaker settlement when we went there early in 1912. He was not a member of the Society of Friends, either birthright or convert, and it was told him directly by his relatives and indirectly by his new associates that in a small town founded by and for a religious group not his own, he could not long last . . . a year at best, before he would be gently frozen out. But Quakers accept with their deliberate philosophy the belief that men should live side by side as brothers, whenever racially and professionally agreeable to the commu-nity, and after a considered and cool look at my father he was allowed to stay. I doubt that he ever let himself be aware of this tacit "permission": *he chose* to be there, to run the *News* and raise his family there, and finally to die there, without any nod except from the Supreme Being. That is how it was, for him.

He appeared to be a decent young man, of seemly habits if somewhat over-tall, and with an occasional wild gleam in his eye (which he soon learned to mask except at home). He had been born into newspapers, and at nine was setting type on a stolen tombstone (still the smoothest surface!) for his father in Iowa villages, while his mother filled up the empty columns of their weekly journal with poems based on Felicia Hemans, and taught

Latin and Greek, and even Anglo-American, in whatever local high school her wandering husband settled near. He was the son of a circuit-rider printer who had been given to publishing excerpts from the sermons of his idol, Peter Cartwright. Grandfather was a giant, very beautiful and subject to violent moods, and after he "saw the light" in his early forties he started tearing down the houses of joy he had once known and building temples to the Lord in their place. So my father knew something of religious fervor when he settled in Whittier, built by a band of outcast Christians for their own peaceable survival.

He went there because the daily paper was for sale at a suspiciously low price. The money he had received for his half of the Albion (Michigan) *Recorder* from his older brother was running out, and so, concurrently, was his wish to leave the newspaper business forever. He had spent most of the cash on options for orange groves near Ventura that proved to be planted on hardpan. He had proved enjoyably that he could never support his family as a beachcomber on Puget Sound. He had discovered in one stint on a paper in San Diego that he was constitutionally unfitted to be anything but his own boss. The editor of the Whittier paper had disappeared, as all non-Quakers there were said to do, and Rex and his good wife, Edith, gave up their wanderings, which she had feared and secretly loathed, and sank all their money and borrowings into the *News*. Her rich disapproving relatives agreed with his local advisers that he could not possibly last in the town and that he was endangering the security of his family. It must have been hard for him to return to a profession he had so much hoped to escape, but after a long life in it he still had the same daring gleam in his eye that was there on his first day at his desk in Whittier. He was still a bungling amateur of orange groves, still superbly convinced of his divine right to be a small-town editor. He believed in predestination, and was a triumphant fatalist.

Edith, when they arrived in Whittier in 1912, seemed well-mannered according to the Quaker ladies who never called on her but managed to observe her closely. She was said to sing well, but unfortunately only at home and in the choir of her heathenish little Episcopal church. She kept having children, which proved that she was at least Christian by intent. But she was said to be of Irish descent. In fact, her mother lived in the same house with her, and although old Mrs. Holbrook dressed and behaved in a proper way, she admitted to having been born somewhere north of Dublin. In other words, both of the ladies living in the big house at the edge of the "nice" part of town must be either Northern Protestants or Southern Papists in their own foreign land, and all Irish females in America were or at least had been cooks.

As for the new young fellow planning to run the *News*, he too bore a name either Irish or Scottish, and most men of his race and build, from what the gentle and withdrawn citizens of Whittier knew, were either cops or rowdy brawlers in saloons, just as fifty years later people with Italian names would be thought of as high-paid killers in things like the Mafia.

All this surmise, as my parents settled blandly or at least doggedly into the little community, was aired now and then at family tables other than ours, and the next day I would pay for it, as the gang of little girls and an occasional sex-hungry boy would trudge behind, while I walked home. We were then between six and ten years old. In the mornings they always stopped at our house, and we walked and hopped together through the quiet sweet-smelling streets, planted with bushes never seen today, and tall hand-some trees brought as seedlings by the courageous homesick pioneers across the Great Desert. Mornings were nice. Afternoons sometimes were a little miserable, but I never let on that I would like to cry or yell. On a bad day, with classes over and the Penn Street schoolyard deserted, I would walk home alone, with my friends of that morning tagging me, perhaps twenty paces behind, like a pack of suddenly captious taunting dogs.

"What does your big fat Irish mother do?" the litany might start.

"My mother takes care of us," I would call back, disdaining to reply to any of the adjectives.

"Oh, no, she doesn't! She's the cook. All Irish women are cooks."

Actually, my mother stayed out of the kitchen as much as possible, except for making divinity fudge perhaps once a year, or an occasional cake like the monument for Father's birthday called a Lady Baltimore, or patting to-gether egg croquettes for the cook to fry in Lent. There was no use explain-ing this to the kids, especially since they kept their distance and it might sound foolish in a shout. So after another half-block, which I paced as fast as possible without seeming to run, and thus satisfy them, somebody would yell, "What does your big skinny Irish father do?"

Again I would let the adjectives slide past me, and yell back that he ran the *News*, and my daylong, yearlong friends would howl with laughter, and shout, "Oh, *no*, he doesn't! He's a cop. All Irish men are cops."

It seems strange to me now, so twisted am I by prejudices and their effects, that this sporadic gibing never really angered me. It did not occur to me to speak of it at home. My friends plainly did not know what they were talking about and would be all right tomorrow. . . . I thought it was part of being there in Whittier, just as other kids in other kinds of ghettos have the same passive acceptance of a lot more of it . . . until they can leave.

There were less than five thousand people in the town then, and only a few of them were anything but Quakers. There were perhaps thirty Episcopalians like us, and then handfuls of other sects, and some Catholics who were mostly Mexican and therefore firmly put outside the city limits in Jim Town. There was one little store run by Jews, called the Bazaar. There was never a Negro, except for our Cynthia who could not long stand her aloneness, even with us to love her. But the people I went to school with were white and they were birthright Friends, and I knew that every morning, any morning, they would stop for me on the sidewalk in front of my house, and speak politely to Mother if she stood on the porch steps, and that then we would tag in a discreetly gamboling pack to the schoolyard, shying loquat or date seeds along the gutters, or green apricots, according to the seasons . . . hopping puddles amicably after it had rained on the lumpy sidewalks. It would be ridiculous to try to prove anything at all to them.

I am not sure what a doctor would say about the apparent passivity on my part, this lack of anger. The teasing was part of life there, completely unimportant as such, and certainly unworthy of my attention. I knew my mother was not a big fat cook and my father not an Irish cop, but our private life was so apart from my friends' that it seemed pointless to try to explain their misconceptions to them.

I think this is true of most children before they emerge from their birth-skins, their spiritual placentas, into active life in the world. I know some of them, now as I did then, from other "restricted areas" as was ours, and I believe that the early years are mostly full of warmth and innocence and love, and that what goes on in cult groups, or on the local Rialto, is mostly unheard, invisible, unjudged, by the little ones. It does not much matter if they are badly housed, nourished by chance, isolated in groups or even alone.

It does not matter until later, when they begin to grow new skins to exist in. Myself, I was well and warmly lodged. But I feel that an equally vulnerable pre-citizen in much less cozy surroundings, and hounded more than I ever was on the sidewalks of no matter what city, will survive if he has love to return to, as I did.

This condition must be unquestioned. Mine was. If there is a confusion in the household or the cave, the child is shaken *there*, and not outside. I stayed unshaken, because my cave was orderly and loving. As I see it now, my father was a strong young man, knowingly plunging himself and his wife and his offspring into a foreign and presumably closed society. She was a tender woman, shaped by her strong Victorian environment, and perhaps as innocent of true ugliness all her life as her little children were for their first years. Together they gave us all we needed to stay unharmed, unpuzzled, for a time.

I never bothered to wonder where my friends heard what they sometimes felt impelled to yell at me, at my younger sister Anne, but it is plain that what they had learned came from the mouths of their parents, people whom many nonmembers of the Friends' Society deem almost saintlike. I knew a lot of them as I grew older. Some were sanctimonious bastards. Some were truly gentle and fine, almost worthy of my parents.

I was never asked inside a Friend's house, in the more than forty years I lived in Whittier. Instead, at least when I was little, all the girls and even a few boys came to our place, freely and often. If we were thirsty, we went through the back porch (Don't tramp into the house and wake Grandmother . . . or the new baby . . . or Mother) for long gasping slurps from a shared tumbler under the kitchen tap. On the way out, we each took an orange from the row of them that always stood on the ledge under the screened window, or an apple or pear in season. If I limited the party to four young ladies, and saw to it that everything was left tidy, I could serve cornflakes and milk on the long piano bench in the living room.

And twice while we lived on Painter Avenue, and then once soon after we moved down to the ranch, Mother gracefully did something for little people she was literally incapable of doing for adults, and gave beautiful, balanced, exciting parties for us. The first was in honor of my birthday, and the last of my sister Anne's, and I forget what brought on the one in the middle, but they were fine routs, attended by all our Episcopal Sunday school associates and many nice Quaker children we knew. By now it is easy to wonder what Mother's motives were, if any. Perhaps she was saying flatly to the other ladies of the little town that we lived in such and such a way and were glad to share it? Certainly she produced the only children's parties in my own experience, and in an uncharacteristic way, and if there were other such celebrations going on in Whittier, we never knew of them.

Occasionally I heard a parent "thee-and-thou" one or another of my friends, but in general this leftover linguistic trait, which had already become a deliberate mannerism, was not used, at least in front of non-Quakers. Of course I was familiar with it, being an Anglican and on close terms with godly language, in which we could be more familiar with our Deity than our dogs. I liked it, and always have, and wish that we could use it again in our family intimacies. In Whittier, the only person who ever said *thee* to me was a tall good-looking widow, highly respected because her own mother had been a minister. She was called Mrs. Osmun. Once she invited me to drive clear to San Gabriel with her and her friend, in a surrey, the only one left in town. I think I was five. Mother let me go.

There was a man along, but I do not remember him except that he took care of the horse. It was a long hot ride, with an occasional automobile whipping past us. The two ladies were swathed in dust-colored clothes and veils, like Mother's when she went riding in our Ford. Almost as often as I would have liked, little boxes and baskets were pulled from under the seats (I rode backwards, as befitted my stature and age and so on), and we ate tepid but delicious dainties. We forded a wide shallow river, perhaps the Rio Hondo. Once in San Gabriel, we could look only from the outside at the old mission and its outbuildings, in spite of the signs begging for visitors, for they were *Catholic*. Then we turned around and headed for home again, and it is interesting that when I finally returned to San Gabriel as a free and much older heathen I felt that I had really been there before, even so tentatively.

The important thing about this first visit—somewhat peculiar if one considers what energy it took to get four people and a horse there and then back again—is that I was called "thee" and "thou" as naturally as leaves floating down a little stream, by the beautiful old Mrs. Osmun. I was a child to her (even if our church was not a *real* one!). It made me feel fine. It sounded right, and this feeling had nothing to do with either religion or semantics.

(Once an older cousin of ours was accepted, as a paying lodger of course, into Mrs. Osmun's large empty house. He stayed there while he worked as a reporter on the *News*, between two somewhat more active sojourns in Greenwich Village, the modish place for all young men from Iowa to go. He has told me that he heard his landlady talking quietly on the telephone with her sister about some proposed purchases in Los Angeles. Mrs. Osmun said firmly, "Well, Susan, thee can bee-ee-tee I wouldn't pay any such price for a footstool!" He said it was as if the Deity were a not-very-bright child; but as a longer resident in the town, I believe that a respectable Quaker lady simply did not use loose terms, such *words*, straight out . . .)

Nobody ever said "thee" to my parents, of course, although after a few decades some men began to call my father by his first name, at least in the right surroundings (Chamber of Commerce meetings, Rotary, the country club . . .). My mother, asocial both by training and because she was personally unsure, remained aloof from people after the first few years of being the loyal young clubwoman wife of the struggling new editor, but she had quiet and lasting affection for two or three of the Quaker ladies, and they for her, although of course she was never invited to drink a cup of tea with them. In fact, the nearest any of us ever came to sharing food with them was the day she died, when Caroline, the banker's eldest daughter, brought us a delicious apple pie, "to help a little, with all the arrangements to make now," as she said sadly.

My sister Anne and I often went into the Friends' church for missionary lectures with Grandmother, when we were little, but I was not invited to "meeting" until I was almost fifty years old . . . and then by a revolutionary member of the Society who was fighting to return to the old simplicity, and do away with things like vested choirs and processionals and such, which were twisting and bedecking the first patterns of worship. As my school friends got to the marrying age I was invited to a few weddings in the big church, and true enough they had a Romish flavor to them, with an unseemly pomp that in our own church would not have surprised me.

When I was still young enough to be forced to take piano lessons, my Quaker teacher was also the organist at her church, and of course I could never have endured the privilege of practicing "In a Persian Market Place" if my family had not been given unwritten approval to employ her, admittedly the only "acceptable" musician in town. After we moved into the country, Mother eased me out of that situation with daring and wiliness, and put me into the much less skilled hands of *our* organist, but her dreams of listening to me ripple through Chopin and Schubert, as she herself had learned to do, were soon broken rudely when the Episcopalian decided, once again, that I was best left thudding through the marketplace.

But how can anyone talk as I do, saying mean things with obvious malice and misinterpretation, about the quiet Quakers, so universally known to be filled with humility, brotherly love, and the general vision of George Fox on the hilltop? In Whittier, perhaps we learned more about that love than was intended, and largely because it never entered into the scheme of things, as such. We were never hurt physically. What is more important, our own culture or lack of it was never questioned or invaded. It was ignored, as long as we behaved ourselves. We, in turn, never thought of trying in any way to "understand" and participate in the religious and social habits of the people we lived with. We were not of their persuasion, which in itself was not exactly friendly but on the other hand was not antagonistic. They in turn had less than no interest in our foreign goings-on in front of our own altars.

The townsmen who very gradually began to call my father Rex, and even to down a nip of his best Scotch after they had played together around the golf course, like good community leaders, were not being Christian, or understanding, or kindly. They simply liked him.

In Whittier we all led our own deliberately separate lives, with mutual respect. The Friends were there first, and if they seemed a little smug it was probably because they still felt, after a few generations, like refugees from a scorned and even persecuted minority group, and what can be more holier-than-thou than a persecuted minority? They had been brave in their flight, and strong and canny in their chosen haven . . .

There were many good kind generous (well, I do not feel sure about that loosely used word, for Rex always said it was like pulling teeth to get money for some of his projects) . . . there were many good and kind people in the town, I know, as well as a few mean cruel ones, and at one time they had the biggest and richest meetinghouse in the Quaker world. I went there with Grandmother to the free missionary shows.

She lived with us, or we with her, or anyway all together after her husband died. She was a smallish woman, compared to my parents, and I often leaned against her in wonderment, to see if there was a single soft place on her firmly encased body. Her cheek might have been one, but it never occurred to me to kiss her. She did not believe in enjoyment, much less joy, and was a rigidly disciplined Puritan from her eighth year until her death at a ripe or at least respectably withered eighty-two. She disbelieved in everything pleasurable, that is, except what was directly connected to Christian Life, preeminently as lived by her fellow Campbellites but peripherally by other white non-Catholics. She believed passionately in clothing and then converting non-whites to her own form of Christianity, except for possible colored Catholics, who would perforce be too damned to succor. That is how and why I went occasionally with her to the grand building where the Friends worshipped, to a missionary show: it would be about bringing faith to the heathen, and therefore it was a duty (never a pleasure) to attend.

Once there were Swiss bell ringers, for some reason, along with a preacher from Palestine who illustrated unforgettably the phrase "My cup runneth over." He poured many too many grains of wheat into a basket instead of a goblet, which I thought would have been more fitting, but it was still a good act, and nobody had to bow his head in prayer, which my granddam approved. (It stuck in her throat to think of her own daughter Edith kneeling and perhaps even genuflecting, in the local outpost of Anglican popery and secondhand mouthings of the Scarlet Woman of Rome.) Grandmother would never have made a good Quaker, being too belligerent of nature, but she appreciated and enjoyed what they offered her as a decent Christian woman, and made no attempt to question them, especially since they would not think of doing so to her. Once more, brotherly love may have hung invisibly in the air of the enormous wooden hall, as the missionary roared and capered, and the stolid musicians tinkled their bells, and we sucked hungrily at the free orange of entertainment.

I sometimes wondered why my school friends, the ones in whose church I sat so happily for these shows, were never there. They went to bed correctly, at the proper time, while I caroused. Dramatic performances were not for Quaker children, and were generally frowned upon in those days by their parents. Perhaps they were offered to us, the "others," a little as Caesar gave circuses to the potentially troublesome Romans, to soothe them. Whatever the motive, my introduction to high-camp entertainment began in the old wooden church, and no amount of later compromise, with vested choirs leading the category, can erase the feeling of friendship and excitement it gave me when I was a child.

My music teacher played there. My friends went there to Sunday school. People rang bells and even water glasses right up there in front, the place where in my own church we were never allowed to set foot or even to kneel, until after Confirmation. Later in my life there would be splashy weddings, and the church would be rebuilt, no longer the biggest Friends' meeting-house in the world but very luxurious and even elegant, and rich of course. (It was then that a few rebels split off and went quietly and often mutely to a room in Whittier College, where they sat together until the Spirit either moved them or did not, and then as silently went home again. They had no need for organists, hymns, ritual . . . and with the smug and even sanctimonious attitude of all religious refugees, they knew themselves to be One with their fathers.)

No bugler blows "Joy to the World" anymore, to the four corners of the town and perhaps the planet. But those were fine Christmas mornings, thanks to the Quakers who let us live in their town in peace. Exactly at seven, from the steeple of the Friends' church, the triumphant blast would come to us, fainter to the north and west and south, and then right into our upstairs sleeping porch, as little Anne and I lay close to Father in the big bed, quivering happily. Soon Mother would be home from singing at Early Service. After breakfast there would be the Tree, even though Grandmother disliked it as a pagan custom, and then we would go up and down the sidewalks of Painter Avenue, and compare dolls and tricycles and wagons with our Quaker peers.

The white children I knew when I was little had no need to be anything but well-fed and secure, in the best houses in a town where they belonged to its best families, the ones with the settlers' names. . . Hadley, Bailey, Newlin, Comstock, Maple. Their ancestors, buried in the Whittier cemetery or along the routes to California, had given up other homes just as solid, positions just as secure, to live their own lives as they saw fit, in a place where they could practice their beliefs unscorned. The settlement they named for their American poet would be theirs, and theirs it was when we came to it.

It still remains a firm core in the sprawling suburb of Los Angeles that was once Whittier, and the part where we lived is now called the Old Town by newcomers of all faiths and races. It is, in its own sedate tree-shaded fashion, just as much a ghetto as was Jim Town down on the river, where most of the Mexicans had to live when I was little. The comfortable old houses like ours have largely been converted into small apartments or doctors' offices. And all around it, in elegant suburbs, and "housing developments" that range from solid to shoddy, and high-rise buildings, live nearly a hundred thousand people. Most of them work in Los Angeles offices or the several great war industries. Freeways make escape quick and easy, and I am told that most people still leave town, as did my own parents, for their frolickings.

Whittier College, which had barely enough young ladies enrolled in it to dance around the Maypole when I first set foot on its campus in 1913 to watch the seemly caperings (another free show!), was definitely worried about overcrowding when I studied there for one semester in 1928, and almost four hundred students bulged out the few buildings on its neat campus. By now it is, in its own contained way, as sprawling as the town, with more than two thousand young people seething discreetly, so far, at its consistent conservatism. It even has an enrollment of fifty or so black students, which one report says is nearly the entire Negro community of the town.

Arithmetically that is surprising, to put it in a correctly gentle and quiet way. It seems to come out as a percentage of one-fortieth of the college student body, and around one two-hundredth of the town's head count. Surely my figures cannot be right, as my fourth-grade teacher at Penn Street would agree from her grave if she could. I do know, though, that our family harbored for a time, too short, the only Negro in Whittier, big Cynthia, who finally left us with mutual hot tears because she was lonely, except for us. She was, in fact, dying, pining, except for us. She was not welcome anywhere, even in the stores. Especially there was no place open for her to worship. The people did not seem to *see* her . . .

Most of those I grew up with in Whittier are gone, either up or down. If some of them still live, they may have forgotten me, as I have many of them. More clearly do I remember their composed remote mothers, always seen from a polite distance, and their quiet fathers, the men who looked over my own sire for several years and then almost smiled at him, as they met in passing on the corner of Greenleaf and Philadelphia. They went to a different church, and never bothered to doubt why. They ate and even dressed differently, because of their conditionings. They recognized good souls and bad, mostly within their own walls. It is probable that they taught all of us more about brotherly love than they realized.

I hope I learned enough about that, in all its forms, while I was a child there in that quiet enclave, to keep me learning more. Some of those forms would not be recognized as love itself, by many of my known and unknown teachers. But every lesson, every lecture listened to, must be interpreted into a personal dialect of the human language, and that is what I keep trying to do. . . .

A *considerable* TOWN

A CONCLUSION

Yes.

Like Mme de Sévigné, I am giddied by "the whole atmosphere . . . the sea, the fortresses, the mountains . . ." And I would *be* there, past, present, future. I would be near the Vieux Port, within sight and feel of it.

One day I found the harbormaster. It took me some time, partly because I did not know his correct title of port captain. I asked at the big Criée on the rive Neuve, and was referred to a couple of small cafés and a chandlery.

The cafés were the kind that fell silent when I went in, first because I was a female foreigner who obviously did not know where she was, and second because I asked a question the people preferred not to answer: Where was the harbormaster? (Later I learned from him that the owners and workers at the public fish auctions were at odds with him, choosing to stay right where they were on the rive Neuve when he wanted to move them up the coast.) The chandlery was run, hopefully for a short time, by a bewildered beautiful young drifter from Rouen or someplace far north, and he fluttered helplessly and then suggested I go across the street to the most important of the yacht clubs, which I did.

It was covered with signs warning me not to set foot in it, but I went up the elegant gangplank and read a dramatic map of the moorings available to the members and a delicious menu for that night's dinner, before I was ushered in and then out of a busy little man's office: he could do nothing for me and knew nothing at all about anything I hoped to learn. (Later I suspected that he too preferred not to recall the harbormaster, whose proletarian opinion that the valuable privately controlled moorings along the quays really belonged to the city of Marseille, for fair taxation anyway, was unpalatable.)

I went off the rive Neuve, up to the rue Sainte, which used to be the road that led Greeks and then Romans to their cemeteries high on the hill where St. Victor was later built. On one of the old buildings I found a grimy brass plate saying something like Reunion Society of Pleasure Boat–Owners, and went into a dark smelly hallway and halfway up the first flight of some rotting narrow stairs before I heard myself telling me to turn around and leave, get out, forget the reason for being in such a foul sinister deserted building. Victorian words like *malodorous, invidious*, were in my head, and when I got back onto the rue Sainte, I felt a childish relief that nobody had heard my steps or run after me, scrabbling ratlike . . . twisted little legs . . . one ear under a straggle of gray hair . . . "Madame, Madame! Come back! Come smile at me . . ."

I walked firmly down to the rive Neuve again, and banged on a couple of locked doors in the bright sunlight, small neat clubhouses for the Bargemen's Union, the Jolly Syndicate of Oars and Anchors. Finally a man in the bait shack at the bend of the rive Neuve into the quai des Belges sent me, correctly enough, to Number Three on the quai du Port.

It was easy, too easy after my various frustrations, right off the far end of the *quai* opposite the little bait shop, and I felt encouraged. But Number Three was a small souvenir store run by an attractive plump woman who explained compassionately to me that the quai du Port *naturally* started at both ends and stopped at the town hall in the middle, or something like that. I would find the harbormaster at Number Three at the other end, she said.

The day was hot and by then I was footweary and there was tomorrow, so I waited for it behind a cool glass of rosé. And in some twenty hours I was at the sea end of the *quai*, a place familiar to me for many years because of the fine small buildings there, which I never even dreamed were occupied by the elusive Captain and his crew. I felt shy about simply walking through the gate by the first of the two matching Italianate pavilions and asking to see the boss, but there had been no apparent way to telephone for an appointment. I pretended I was a young, eager, beautiful girl-reporter in a TV serial . . .

The buildings are lovely, especially from across the Port: low, graceful. The first was built in 1719, to house the officials of the Health and Sanitation works, and its twin sister was added in the nineteenth century. There is a famous statue of St. Roch over the gateway, erected to protect Marseille against the Plague, "Scourge of Provence." It is perhaps more a symbol of blind faith than of terror by now, but well repaired after an American corvette knocked it down while maneuvering up to the *quai* for a medical inspection in 1839. There used to be important carvings and paintings inside, mostly about health and sanitation, of course (i.e., disease and sewage . . .), but they have been moved to better housing, and by 1973 when I went to meet the harbormaster, the large light rooms were sparsely furnished, very clean, with a few bright posters and blown-up photographs of the Vieux Port on their walls, and the tall graceful windows wide open. (In 1976 all the business was located on a large square floating dock, while the fine old pavilions underwent restoration as valuable historical architecture.)

At first I thought nobody worked there. It was as quiet as a country garden-house. Then a lone young man spotted my obvious confusion about where to find the Captain behind one of the unmarked open doors, and when I told him why I was there he conferred somewhere. The hall I was in was bare and airy, and a bee buzzed in and then out onto the waterfront. I could hear a typewriter somewhere, tapped hesitantly. The clerk beckoned to me, and I went into a big, almost naked office where he introduced me to Captain Agostelli and then left.

The harbormaster was a tall, square man, more like a Northerner than a Marseillais except for his dark eyes. He was courteous in a gruff way, and reminded me of Inspector Maigret, which I finally told him. That seemed to please him very much. I soon stopped trying to be a bright, scared news-

of this fine old port. In New York, where I worked with the Port Authority for more than a year, learning, learning, every inch dockside is privately owned and paid for. Therefore rents and taxes are completely controlled. Here in Marseille everything is now in the hands of the city, and supposedly the people, and is therefore corrupt and ill-managed."

I felt almost uneasy at his candid vehemence, for posters from the last elections were still peeling off the town walls, and I knew who owned the local newspapers and a little of what the town fathers were promising. He was indiscreet.

"Do you know the Société Nautique du Lacydon?" he asked, thumping his desk the way an impatient bull will paw the ground when nobody is looking. His face was red.

I told him that I looked down on it from where I lived above St. Victor: a neat small "marine" filled with pleasure boats. He snorted. "That was an enormous job, all footed by the City of Marseille, with no repayment of any kind demanded for the first three years, and with memberships in what amounts to a rich private club selling for huge sums that go into the club itself! Who owns it? Is the city collecting any taxes? And who paid for it? It cost us millions, I tell you!"

He stood up and loosened his collar and sat down again. "I learned a lot in New York," he said mildly. "And what do you think of our sewage? This was once the foulest port in the Western world."

I told him that it smelled fairly clean to me . . . compared, for instance, to the East River around the docks in New York. Of course, I said cautiously, there were always bits of rubbish brushing against the quai des Belges before the garbage-sweep sucked them up . . . especially after a holiday . . .

He said, "There again! The government! The town! In 1837 several studies were made of how to swill out this bucket, after the City had organized a futile system of pontoons with scoops and so on, but the State declined to mix in what it called 'a local problem.' And here we are, known worldwide as the filthiest, most stinking port in the world! We had one little scow that went around, called *Marie-Salope*, Mary the Slut. By 1857 the port was so filled with silt that even she could not navigate well, and the pollution was incredible. We were getting about 150 liters of filthy water a second, to flush out a port with an overall water surface of some 27,000 square meters! Then in 1850 Longchamps brought us the clean water of the Durance, a steady flow of more than a thousand liters a second." He stood up again, tightened his tie, and said, "We still have *Marie-Salope* on duty. The open pipes are connected to a main one that dumps away from shore, and the household garbage is carted off to Le Crau, but . . . no doubt New York has its problems too."

"No doubt," I said. He sat down just before I stood up to thank him and go. He looked strong and unruffled. "There is always something interesting going on here," he said chattily. "Perhaps you could help me with a little problem . . ."

I could not keep from laughing, and it was then that I told him he reminded me very much of Simenon's Inspector Maigret. He looked enormously pleased, and almost smirked as he leaned back and said, "I should be puffing at a pipe! Well, the come-and-go of yachts here is really much too casual for my own comfort, and I have one sticky little situation on my hands right now that involves one of your countrymen. You know that when a skipper comes in, he shows me his passport, but no note is made of it here?"

"We have to in hotels," I interrupted, and he said, "Yes, but not in ports. It is careless, all right, but it's a French tradition. And an American with an odd name, something like Hirsh Guinafrom, from some little town in perhaps New Jersey, docked here about ten months ago, complete with a crew of one beautiful dame, and showed me a passport, which I returned to him, and then he disappeared. He and the woman simply vanished.

"In about six months I began to get a lot of complaints from other boat-owners about the dangerous condition of the abandoned yacht, and I wrote to the town in America. Answer: 'Person Unknown.'"

I felt as if I were reading the last book off the Presses de la Cité, with Maigret across the desk from me instead of his Marseille sibling. I suggested in a rather ambiguous way that the local American Consul would probably be able to verify the name and address if such a passport still existed, or even if it did not. The name did not sound quite right, I said.

Agostelli sighed as if he were tired, weary, exhausted. "Perhaps it will have to come to that," he muttered. But I could see that he much preferred to let the unwelcome deserted boat rot or burn or sink, or break loose and drift out to sea . . .

We looked appreciatively at each other, he because I had told him he reminded me of a mutual hero, and I because he was a pleasant person, and after my thanks I left the bright, salty air of his office with regret. I was glad I had tracked him down.

On the way home, around the three sides of the Vieux Port, I felt at ease, perhaps more than ever before. There were things I missed: the jugglers at Christmastime in the fifties; my children then; the man I called Bacchus who for a while in the sixties sold shells marked "Coastal," "Local," "Exotic," while he looked peacefully at the port and drank five or six liters a day of dark red wine; the strangest beggar of my whole life in the doorway of the old church sinking into the marshes of the Lacydon.

He was perhaps the last of the great army of professional mendicants who once almost ruled the town of Marseille, and occupied the Vieille Charité and directed the funerals and weddings of the helpless citizens with their threats and payments. He lay motionless and soundless, comatose, in rain and blazing heat, one leg cut off, hardly a living thing except for a small trickle of urine that now and then seeped out. Someone must have come at night to pile him onto a cart and take him away until the next morning, and dump a few coins out of the old mariner's cap that lay by him all day. It was hard to look at him, except as a once-man, until the day when I made myself see past his bloated face, past his one leg, past his thin red hair, and he opened his bright pale blue eyes and gazed straight at me, and I knew who he was.

Twenty years and fifteen years before, he had been the strong bold Gypsy-boy in Aix, a jaunty gimpy with a crutch and blazing hair, and red-haired, blue-eyed babies by every little skinny Gypsy-girl in town. He had swung boldly up and down the cours Mirabeau, never begging, but watching his girl-women at their trades. I had seen him since he was perhaps fourteen, when he already had one small girl pregnant and proud.

He looked fully at me, and I at him, because he knew exactly who I was. I felt shaken. The recognition was ageless. Then his eyes closed, and he was a bag of rotted rags and bones, and I went down the quay past the bus stop to Aix, knowing that I had touched Time on the sleeve.

Perhaps that is what makes it essential that I be in Marseille, to stay in active contact with immortality now and then. It is not necessary to have a dead man look into my eyes, any more than it is to talk with a fine healthy port captain or watch my children skip carefully between the long nets laid out to be mended, tomorrow or twenty years ago. But how can I know, otherwise?

As They Were

PREFACE

In the sixties, my fine old house in St. Helena seemed hollow, with the children gone. I said, Mary Frances, now is the time to go to new places and find different views of things.

Friends kept the hearth warm and the animals happy, and other friends let me stay in their own places when they were away. It was a vivid period of slow wandering, very rich, like a carpet I had often trod before I realized that it was there.

One winter I went to Long Island to a house I knew well from several summer visits. It was on the dunes near Bridgehampton. There was a car, so that I could drive into the village for mail and food. I cashed checks at the liquor store next to the grocery. I liked the tough fellow there, and when I went back after several months in Sag Harbor, I liked him even more, because he laughed with real pleasure when he saw me, and said, "God, were we glad to get you off the dunes and outta here!"

I knew why, because he was one of the volunteer firemen who would have risked their lives to reach the house if they knew I was without heat or help. They did not want to die, any more than I did, but . . .

The story I wrote about that incident is called "The Wind-Chill Factor," and the house I lived alone in, except for rare weekends with its owner who came down from her job in New York, was a deliberate contradiction of the local wisdom: "natives" of that part of the island build and farm and work *inland*. Only ignorant summer people stay along the blandly beautiful beaches, flirting in bland ignorance with hurricanes and such blandly lethal happenings.

My house had been partly demolished in the last Big Blow, but was solid again and partly "winterized," as was then said, and my hostess and I agreed that I was indeed a lucky person to face a cozy winter there. I holed in.

After what I reported in "The Wind-Chill Factor," I knew that many more lives than mine depended on whether my lights had gone off, those three or four wild nights, and I moved to a one-room flat in Sag Harbor. I had the parlor and bathroom of what had once been a whaler captain's house, with a cursory kitchenette at one end. I was warm and quiet, and worked steadily because there was nothing else to do. Outside, everything was mostly silence, because the snow stayed high for weeks at a time, and it was arduous to shuffle down the narrow high tunnels of sludge that led to the post office and the grocery store.

Fortunately, right across from my lodging was a small boozerie owned by a handsome Greek who was paraplegic from a railroad accident. We talked nostalgically about good wines, and I came to enjoy and even appreciate popular jug-stuff.

I never capitulated to the currently popular fizz wines, carbonated mixtures of fruit juices and dregs, but through the thin back wall into the apartment that had once been the captain's dining room I often listened to a young fisherman, laid off during the bad weather, drink himself worse than silly on something like Thunderhead or Tango-Tango and then commit conjugal rape on his very devout wife every Saturday night, so that she could not receive Communion the next morning, after her Saturday Confession. Ho hum. Their baby, about six months old, wailed a lot. They lived in a somewhat smaller "parlor" than mine, and there was always that half-gallon jug handy, under the bed.

My Greek friend and I talked in a detached casual way about this.

"The Wind-Chill Factor" taught me that there is a difference between what is true and what one believes is the truth. I depicted the storm in as bare a way as I could, since it had happened only to *me*. During the strange ordeal, there was nobody else, to observe or even survive. It was a true catharsis.

For a few days, after it, I felt floaty and emptied. And I had to face the fact that all my vague plans to write about an earlier life were crude fabrications of a fertile and fairly articulate mind. I wanted suddenly to write about *my* first years, for some unknown pushing reason, and I saw, after the wind on the dunes, that nobody but a child can write what has just happened to him. It is almost impossible for an older person to report such things without coloring them, twisting, invading the story, to make a more vivid or more self-flattering report.

In Sag Harbor I was almost always alone, for the months I was there. I never felt *lonely*, though, because that is not my bent. Some might say my life was austere. With an occasional glass of California jug-rosé from the little icebox that hummed along in a corner of my room, I tried to go as far back as I could into the life I honestly believed I had lived when I was four, or even ten. (I was writing *Among Friends*, although I did not know it then.)

It was a sweaty job, at times painful, but since the time on the dunes, and then in Sag Harbor, I know that I can never write polite tomfoolery again, if I ever did.

sister Age

FOREWORD

St. Francis sang gently of his family: his brother the Sun, his sister the Moon. He talked of Brother Pain, who was as welcome and well-loved as any other visitor in a life filled with birds and beasts and light and dark. It is not always easy for us lesser people to accept gracefully some such presence as that of Brother Pain or his cousins, or even the inevitable visits of a possibly nagging harpy like Sister Age. But with a saint to guide us, it can be possible.

This story about the portrait of Ursula von Ott, a forgotten German or Swiss lady, may seem odd as an introduction to a collection of stories about aging and ending and living and whatever else the process of being human is about. I know, though, that my devastated old piece of painted leather, half eaten by oil-hungry insects when it was already worn with years, has been a lodestar in my life.

Before I found the picture in a junk-shop in Zurich, in about 1936, I was writing of old people who had taught me things I knew I needed, in spite of my boredom and impatience. And years later, after I had sent away the boxes of notes made in the several decades since I first met Ursula, I realized that all this time when I had thought I was readying myself to write an important book about the art of aging, I had gone on writing stories about people who were learning and practicing it long before I was.

Sometimes we met for only a few seconds. Probably the old Bible salesman who stumbled to our door at the ranch did not remember me five minutes later, but he was the one who first taught me that people can cry without a sound, and without knowing why. It was a valuable lesson, and as mysterious now as it was when I was about twelve, watching him walk slowly out to the dusty road again, and feeling the cool new tears run down my cheeks. And I forgot it, for about thirty years.

Sometimes the meetings with Sister Age's messengers are long, tedious, even unwitting. For instance, I knew my father's father for almost twenty years, but we never really met, and certainly did not recognize each other as appointed teacher or pupil. By now I sometimes regret this, because I see him as possessing great strength and dignity that were mine for the taking. I doubt, though, that he felt much more interest in me than I in him. We were as impersonal as two animals of different sex and age but sharing some of the same blood, unaware that we lifted our hooves in a strangely similar way as we headed for the same hay-mangers, the same high hills. Even now I cannot feel any strong reason for making notes about him. But I may, I may.

Certainly there were violent flashlike meetings, all my life, with people much older than I, of different colors and sexes and social positions, who left marks to be deciphered later. This was the case with the Bible salesman: I did not think consciously of him for a long time (Why should I?), when suddenly I knew that I must add some words about him to the boxes of notes . . .

The art of aging is learned, subtly but firmly, this way. I wrote fast, to compress and catch a lesson while I could still hear it, and not because it had happened to *me*, so that *I* was recording it, but because it was important to the whole study. It was, for the time I made the notes anyway, as clear as ringing crystal that such hints are everywhere, to be heeded or forever unheard by the people who may one day be old too.

So all the notes I took were caught on the run, as it were, as I grew toward some kind of maturity. I never thought of them as anything but clinical, part of the whole study of aging that Ursula von Ott was trying to help me with. I kept on checking dates and places and events, not at all about my own self but simply as a student in a class, preparing a term paper and leaving scraps that might be useful to other workers in the same field.

By now some of my notes sound like fabrications, invented to prove a point in an argument. This is because it is my way of explaining, and it has always been a personal problem, even a handicap. When I tell of a stubbed toe or childbirth or how to serve peacocks' tongues on toast it sounds made-up, embroidered. But it is as it happened to *me*.

This may explain why I have spent my life in a painstaking effort to tell about things as they are to me, so that they will not sound like autobiography but simply like notes, like factual reports. They have been set down honestly, to help other students write their own theses.

And now my very long, devoted collecting is over. The reports are stored in some academic cellars for younger eyes to piece together, perhaps. The stories that stayed behind are mostly about other people than myself, and may at least prove that I have been listening for clues that Frau von Ott has tried to show me. Some of them may be useful, in moments of puzzlement as to what to do next in our inevitable growth.

So, with the usual human need for indirection, I introduce my Sister. St. Francis might call her, in a gentle loving way, Sister Age. I call her my teacher, too.

The first time I met Ursula, and recognized her as a familiar, I was walking with Tim down a narrow street off the main bridge in Zurich.

Tim was to die a few years later, except in my heart, and Zurich was a cold secret city in Switzerland in 1936, and probably still is. We were there because we lived near Vevey and Tim was silently involved with some of the Spanish fighters living in Zurich during the "revolution" in their country.

We were innocent to look at, and Tim was useful in getting drawings and paintings out of war-wracked Spain, and I was strangely adept at drinking good coarse wine from a skin held far from my open mouth and then keeping it firmly shut, while all the men talked in the small dim cellar-cafés. We were treated with care. I was greeted politely and then put into a corner, with an occasional squirt of *roja* to remind me of true Spanish courtesy, while the schemings went on in more languages than Spanish and French and German.

At home again, we did not talk much about these smoky meetings, but usually they meant that Tim would be away from Vevey for a few days, always carrying a tightly rolled umbrella, like any proper Anglo-Saxon gentleman. Four or five years later, there was a big exhibition in Geneva, of treasures secreted from the Prado, and it was odd to walk past etchings and even small canvases that had come into Switzerland inside that bumbershoot, that prim old gamp . . .

So . . . one day Tim and I were walking down a narrow street in the old part of Zurich. There was a small shop ahead of us: junk, castoffs, rummage. There were a couple of bins of rags and a table of shabby books outside. Two or three empty picture frames leaned against the dirty glass of the dim window, and Tim stopped to look at them because he might be able to clean them to use for some of his own drawings. A man shuffled out of the shop, impatient to get rid of two tourists before he might have to turn on his lights for them.

And I saw the picture of Ursula, Sister Age. It was behind the old frames, and I pulled it out rudely, fiercely, so that Tim was surprised. In the twilight it seemed to blaze at me, to call strongly a forceful greeting.

I said, "We must get this."

Tim looked quickly at the dirty old picture and then at me. "All right if you say so. But we can't take it along to the meeting."

The junk-man said, "If you buy it you take it. I don't keep it."

I said, "Of course. I'll take it now, back to the hotel. I'll meet you at the café, Tim." I knew that he needed me, to add to the bland casual touristlook the Spaniards seemed to want for whatever they were planning.

"No. We have time," he said, because he recognized the abrupt necessity in me, and we left the junk-man staring with surprise at the money in his hand, and hurried down to the bridge in silence. Under a streetlight Tim took the picture and looked at it and asked me what had happened, and I tried to tell him that it was the book I was going to write. What book? When? How did I know? I felt irked, as if we both had always known all about it, although it had just been born wordlessly in front of the drab little shop.

I was going to write about growing old, I told this dear man who would not. I was going to learn from the picture, I said impatiently. It was very clear to me, and I planned to think and study about the art of aging for several years, and then tell how to learn and practice it.

One fine thing about Tim was that although, a lot of the time, he thought I was funny, he never laughed when I was not. So that evening as we ran on over the bridge above the thick rushing water, he said seriously Yes and You are right and Get busy . . . things like that. We stopped again under a strong streetlight, and in it the remote, monkey-sad eyes of the old woman stared far past us from the picture as she thought perhaps about a letter in her dropped hand. Her face was quiet, but ugly veins stood out on her thin arm, as if her blood ran too fast for comfort.

"She will make a wonderful cover for the book . . . rich, dark, rewarding," I said.

"She's an ugly old lady," Tim said. "That moustache. She looks like a monkey, all right . . . that long lip, and melancholy eyes."

"Yes. She's removed from it, from all the nonsense and frustration. She's aloof and real. She's past vanity."

Tim said the book cover was already a fait accompli. Why not? "Go ahead," he said. "Get busy."

Neither of us questioned the strange unemotional decision that had been made, and after another wine-fed smoky night in Zurich Tim went away for a few days, and I waited in Vevey and looked long and deeply at the picture. It hung above my desk, as it was to do in many other climates, on its strong leather thong, and every time I looked at the old face, she reminded me of what I would do.

The picture is painted on leather, stretched clumsily on a heavy frame of unmitred fruitwood, about nineteen inches by twenty-five. It is awkwardly executed, in thick rich oils, by a fairly well-tutored young man full of romanticism and fashionable disdain. He was provincially worldly, probably the pampered son of affluent merchants, filled with the stylish yearnings of his peers in 1808. His work is cluttered with leaves and drooping boughs, an ornate marble pedestal carrying his stark white bust, small canvases of amorous conquests in his young life, always with the same beautiful hero lying like a half-clad exhausted child between ripe rosy thighs of uniformly blonde goddesses.

Of course his memorial bust is handsomer than any living youth could look; his neck is longer, his nostrils flare wider, his lips curl in a more fashionable sensuality than any mortal's could, even in 1808 in a provincial burg like Frankfurt or Zurich or Bonn. It is all a fine dream, down to the pinkest fattest cupids born to hold up his nonchalant sketches of a would-be rake's progress from leg to leg or at least lap to lap of every available Venus, all exactly alike in his plainly limited field of pursuit. And the flowers that climb and twine are his own favorites, all in full bloom at once to symbolize his eternal loss. The flags in bold bas-relief on the pedestal are from the stylish regiment he may or may not have joined, and there are bold hints of more than a couple of noble family crests, in case he might marry well before taking off in search of Napoleon and glory.

Another dimmer pedestal to the far left in the picture is doubtless meant for his mother's urn, when her long empty life has finally wept itself to a close. It is crudely made, with plaster crumbling off, and a few bricks showing. There are no escutcheons or regimental flags to ennoble it. It is as plain and ugly, by stern design, as the old woman who waits to escape to a shabby urn atop it, in the shadows of the fine marble monument to her brave son.

And suddenly this angry and impatient adolescent becomes, for one moment, a painter. He learned the rudiments of perspective on a tour of the Greek Isles with his tutor in 1805, and his political caricatures titillated his classmates at the local gymnasium in 1807, and then for a few seconds in Time, he seized the image of Sister Age herself. He was too blinded by ignorance of himself and his model and Life to see anything but the cruel cartoon of a once-beautiful bitch turned into a lorn crone abandoned to her grief. He did everything ugly he could, in his escape: her lined face is like pallid clay, with a full moustache and even the shadows of a shaven underlip. The one eye showing in half-profile is red-rimmed and shrunken, and her large ear is plebeian: pink, swollen, revolting, with its full lobe promising a hellishly long life. Her hair is gray and thin, topped with a tiny round black cap like a rabbi's but with two gold leaves on it to prove something like her Christian gentility. Her gaze is remote, behind her big masculine nose (*his* nose, but meant for a hero, not an old biddy . . .).

On the back of the painted leather, in strong black characters, is a legend in surprisingly schoolboyish German, that says it is a picture of Ursula von Ott, born in 1767, the mother of several sons, the last of whom has created, before leaving for the battlefield in 1808, this forecast of his death and the inevitable loneliness of his bereaved parent.

So here is the picture of Ursula that for so long hung above my desk or over my bed, speaking to me about life and death, more than I thought there was to learn. Tim never laughed at me, and nobody ever questioned the ugly dark old picture hanging by its crude thong on walls in Switzerland and then wherever else we were. It was a part of the whole, like wine or air.

I began to clip things I read about aging, because I felt that the picture was teaching me. I thought all the time, in a kind of subliminal fashion, about the anger and blind vision of youth, and the implacable secret strength of the old. I thought about human stupidity. It began to be a family joke, but not a foolish one, to transport my boxes of "information," as we moved here and there.

In perhaps 1970, long after too short a life with Tim, during which he subtly taught me how to live the rest of it without him, I found that for the first time since I was about two years old I was without commitments, responsibilities, dependents, emotional ties, and suchlike traps. I decided to look at some familiar places, to see if they were new again. I closed a few boxes of clippings, to keep them from wind and dust, rubbed the painting of Ursula with good oil on both sides of the leather, and left. (Perhaps it is odd that I never thought of returning to Zurich.) I had gone away many times since Tim died, and had always put oil on the picture, so that its dream of weeping willow leaves and fat Venuses and Ursula's moustache would be alive and ready to welcome me back again.

This time, though, there was what I can only think of as an accident in Time. Silverfish, beautiful elusive predators, devoured most of the pigments on the ripe old leather, and then much of that too, so that held up to the light it is translucent, like dirty lace . . . except for one part . . .

Ursula is still there. The omnivorous insects did not touch her. The striped respectable costume, the black cap on her thin gray hair, are all there. Her resigned stocky body still lays one hand with firm dignity on the pedestal under the bust, although the marble is shadowy. Her other skinny arm still hangs, swollen veins and all, against her skirts, and she holds listlessly the letter telling of her noble son's death. Her sad eyes, always tearless, look brighter than before.

There are still hints of drooping faded boughs and blossoms, but all the voluptuous rosy goddesses in their lush draperies, in their golden frames propped up by fluttering cupids, and all the pictures of their young hero lying between their knees, and even all the crossed regimental flags and carved escutcheons are gone, digested by a million silent bugs. Nothing is left but Ursula von Ott, and the picture that was meant to be a cruel caricature painted in youthful frustration by a sentimental boy may well be final proof that even the least of us is granted one moment of greatness.

Nobody can know now whether Ursula's son came back from his dream of heroism and noble death and became a good Swiss burgher. All I can see is what he, and Time, and the silverfish have left for me: the enigmatic, simian gaze of a woman standing all alone. She is completely alive in a landscape of death, then and now. She does not need anything that is not already within her, and the letter of information hangs useless. Above her big strong nose, above the hairy shadows around her subtly sensuous mouth, her eyes look with a supreme and confident detachment past all the nonsense of wars, insects, birth and death, love . . .

After too long a time to look at her, I finally knew that I had filled too many boxes with clippings about Old Age. I stopped thinking that I would write a book about the art of aging. (Ursula von Ott was teaching me humility.) I gave away all the boxes of notes and clippings. (She was teaching me how to be simpler.) Finally . . .

And here I would like to say *then* or *last night* or even *this morning*, I built a good fire, and broke up the brittle old leather, and burned it and the fruitwood frame and watched them consume and curl themselves into pale ash. But I cannot. (There is more to listen to, more to learn from the old lady . . .)

The picture is beside me, leaning against a bookcase. Its leather thong is long since broken, and all that comes out to my eyes from the dark lacy background is the vivid figure of an aging woman with a little velvet cap on her sparse hair. She ignores the doomful letter with its once-red seal, and the once-fine marble bust, and the once-mockingly pretty pictures of venal pleasures and wishful trappings of a forgotten life. She waits, superbly aloof and untroubled.

She is my teacher and my sister, and will tell me more, in due time.

AFTERWORD

Of course it was strange to send away some forty years of accumulated clippings and notes and even lengthy writings that I had kept since my first meeting with Ursula von Ott, Sister Age, in Zurich. There were a lot of books by other people too, everything from Simone de Beauvoir's lengthy documents about the aging process, to slim tacky collections of written "thoughts" by therapy-groups of senior citizens in small Texas towns. I felt surgically bewildered as the cartons went off to their chosen resting-place, as if I'd had more than my limbs amputated. I wondered why my breath still kept going in and out, why my truncated mind still clicked. What had all these readings taught me? What was left?

Surely, I kept saying with some doggedness, I had learned a truth or two from my long ponderings and considerings about the condition most of us animals and plants must bow to. Had I found nothing worth the decades of such compulsive study? I felt lost and somewhat foolish.

By now, several years after I turned my back on all this, I think that I know a few things more clearly than I did when I was young, long before Ursula helped me pull my fumblings into focus.

I know, for instance, that I like old people, when they have aged well. And old houses with an accumulation of sweet honest living in them are good. And the timelessness that only the passing of Time itself can give to objects both inside and outside the spirit is a continuing reassurance.

I have formed a strong theory that there is no such thing as "turning into" a Nasty Old Man or an Old Witch. I believe that such people, and of course they are legion, were born nasty and witchlike, and that by the time they were about five years old they had hidden their rotten bitchiness and lived fairly decent lives until they no longer had to conform to rules of social behavior, and could revert to their original horrid natures.

This theory is hard to prove, because by the time a person begins to show his trueborn nature, most of the people who knew him when he was little have either died or gone into more immediate shadows. I still believe that it is probable, however. I have lived long enough to keep a sharp eye on a few of my peers, and they bear out almost frighteningly the sad natures they first promised us to end with.

On the other hand, there are a lot of people who seem to be born merry or serene or very lively. They are happy vital little babies and children, whether they live in ghettos or in suburban villas surrounded by electronic security systems. They need only one thing in life besides food and shelter, and that is warm open love from some person or animal or thing in their surroundings. They often live until they are very old, through the same delights and sadnesses that everyone else does, but after all the years of social subterfuge and conniving they emerge as bright souls . . . not nasty, not bitchy, just *good*.

If I could choose, I would like that to happen to me, because in our culture it is difficult to be old, and still live with younger fellowmen, and it helps to be tolerably acceptable instead of boring or obnoxious. So far, myself, I think I am in luck, because I was a lively, healthy child who wanted and got a great share of affection. I notice that as I get rid of the protective covering of the middle years, I am more openly amused and incautious and less careful socially, and that all this makes for increasingly pleasant contacts with the world. (It also compensates for some of the plain annoyances of decrepitude, the gradual slowing down of physical things like muscles, eyes, bowels. In other words, old age is more bearable if it can be helped by an early acceptance of being loved and of loving.)

The physical hindrances are of course important, no matter how little an old person manages to admit their dominance. As I write this I am well into my seventies, and I think that I have aged faster than I meant to, whatever that means! (It means, for one thing, that I resent being stiff and full of creaks and twinges.) I did not plan to be the way I am, although I probably knew more than most of my peers about the inevitabilities of disintegration. Fortunately, though, because I met Sister Age so long ago, I can watch my own aging with a detachment she has taught me. I know about the dismays and delights of my condition, and wish that all of us could prepare ourselves for them as instinctively and with as much outside help as we do those of puberty, adolescence, pregnancy, menopausal and climacteric changes . . .

The aging process is a part of most of our lives, and it remains one we try to ignore until it seems to pounce upon us. We evade all its signals. We stay blandly unprepared for some of its obnoxious effects, even though we have coped with the cracked voices and puzzling glands of our emerging natures, and have been guided no matter how clumsily through budding love-pains, morning-sickness, and hot flashes. We do what our mentors teach us to do, but few of us acknowledge that the last years of our lives, if we can survive to live them out, are as physically predictable as infancy's or those of our full flowering. This seems impossible, but it is true.

We are helped by wise parents and teachers and doctors to live through our first couple of decades, and then to behave more or less like creative, productive social creatures, and then to withdraw from the fray, if possible on our various kinds of laurels. And then what?

We are unprepared for the years that may come as our last ones. We are repelled and frightened by our physical changes, some of them hindering and boring, and we feel puzzled and cheated.

Plainly, I think that this clumsy modern pattern is a wrong one, an ignorant one, and I regret it and wish I could do more to change it. Ours is not a society that can accept with patience the presence of clumsy or inept or slow-spoken human beings, and just as untrained puzzled young people drift aimlessly through our slums, untrained puzzled old men and women wait to die in rest homes everywhere. The statistics of a Beauvoir tome are as monotonous as the outcries of sensational journalism: there is no room, right now in our society, for the useless.

That does not mean, though, that some of us who seem meant to survive *need* do it blindly. I think we must use what wits we have, to admit things like the fact that it is harder to get up off the floor at seventy than at fourteen . . . or even forty. We must accept and agree with and attend to with dispassion such things as arthritis, moles that may be cancerous, constipation that may lead to polyps and hernias, all the boring physical symptoms of our ultimate disintegrations. (Old clocks tick more slowly than they did when young.)

What is important, though, is that our dispassionate acceptance of attrition be matched by a full use of everything that has ever happened in all the long wonderful-ghastly years to free a person's mind from his body . . . to use the experience, both great and evil, so that physical annoyances are surmountable in an alert and even mirthful appreciation of life itself.

This sounds mawkish and banal as I try to write it, but I believe it. I am glad that I have been able to live as long as I have, so that I can understand why Ursula von Ott did not weep as she stood by the funeral urn of her son, surrounded by all the vivid signs of his short silly life . . . the fat cupids, the fatter Venuses whose satiny knees he lolled against. She did not smile, but behind her deep monkey-eyes she surely felt a reassuring warmth of amusement, along with her pity that he never had tried to feel it too.

Parts of the aging process are scary, of course, but the more we know about them, the less they need be. That is why I wish we were more deliberately taught, in early years, to prepare for this condition. It would leave a lot of us freed to enjoy the obvious rewards of being old, when the sound of a child's laugh, or the catch of sunlight on a flower petal is as poignant as ever was a girl's voice to an adolescent ear, or the tap of a golf ball into its cup to a balding banker's.

When I was about twelve, my grandmother died and we all relaxed, especially at table. She was puritanical by nature, and did not believe in the indulgences of the flesh, so that sitting lazily after a good meal was not our privilege until she left us. Then we were like mice, with the cat gone. One day, after a long Sunday lunch, my younger sister and I stayed at table with our parents in the cool dining room. We were quiet, full of sponge cake and peace. Mother murmured toward the end of the table where her husband sat. They sipped glasses of port from the decanter that usually stood untouched on the sideboard. Mother said idly something about Old Mrs. Tolbert, the organist at church. "I do wish she would stop scratching herself," she said. Father said, just as lazily and with as little malice, "Maybe she doesn't take enough baths." His wife protested gently, with a soft shrug and a little grimace. I said, with some boldness because although Anne and I were invited to stay on at the table now and then, we still spoke only when spoken to, as in Grandmother's recent days, "No. It's because she itches."

My parents put down their glasses. Anne looked daringly at me, although with correct politeness because of where we were.

"No," I said again. "She is old, and old people itch."

"Ah?" Mother asked, and Father went on, "Is that so? What do you think you mean?"

I said, "Well, I think the skin gets drier when people start to wither. You can see old women's arms. And when the skin gets withery, it itches. And anyway, they don't know they are scratching. They aren't dirty. They may just need to be oiled."

Anne said, "Scratching is rude. It's disgusting."

"I think so too," Mother said. "Disgusting. Old Mrs. Tolbert is really . . ." She sipped the last of her wine, and Father tipped his glass back and stood up. "Now that we've had our little lesson in geriatrics," he said, "and know all about how we'll itch as we age, I suggest that our medical adviser and her sister clear the table and leave us to our own pursuits. I may rub a little lotion on my chin, or—"

Mother laughed and we all went our ways on that fine free Sunday afternoon. But I knew I was right about Mrs. Tolbert. I did not like her, because she had a strong smell, but it was plain that she could not help her scratching: she was drying up like an old shoe and needed to be waxed. She did not need soap and water. Anne and I went on talking about this, as we tidied the kitchen before the cook came back from her Sunday cavortings. We decided that baths are all right, even fun, but that old people need *oil* on their skins, just as new babies do . . . olive oil, or maybe Hinds' Honey and Almond Cream, our current dream of exotic ointments.

And I kept on thinking about old people, and writing notes about them, and readying my spirit to meet Ursula von Ott on that dank crooked street in Zurich. Then, for decades, I kept on clipping and writing some of the notes that are in this book, instead of in a weighty set of statistics on library reference shelves. In one way or another they are about *why* Ursula was not weeping as she held the notice of her son's brave death in her slack old hand, and perhaps of why Old Mrs. Tolbert would have been better off with oil instead of soap and water on her itchy skin.

The crux of it all, perhaps the real secret, is that there was nobody to rub the gentle oil into Mrs. Tolbert's itch. She was alone, and unprepared to be so. There are too many people like her, caught unready for their last days, unprepared to cope with the logistics of dignified acceptance. She forgot to bathe now and then, forgot that she was scratching herself in front of finicky observers . . . finally forgot to breathe. There was nobody in the world to help her.

Mrs. Tolbert possibly started me on my long ponderings about how hard it can be for lonely old people to stay sweet, much less give a small damn whether they are or not. And her common plight leads neatly into the saddest conclusion I have reached about the art of aging, which can and should be as graceful and generally beneficent a "condition" as any other in our lives.

Our housing is to blame. It is said that by the end of this century most citizens in the Western world will have adapted themselves to living as family units in allotted spaces no bigger than a modern compact car. There will be at least four people to each cubicle: two parents and, temporarily at least, two children. (This social phenomenon is already well developed in Japan, where too many active healthy humans manage to live highly disciplined lives in too little space. Westerners will take longer to accept such an inevitability, and learn to adapt to its paranoidal side effects.)

There will be well-designed patterns for our prospective quarters, at least for sleeping, and hygiene will perforce be almost as necessary as oxygen, to avoid epidemics of everything from disease to civil mayhem. Bathing will probably be in communal centers, as will most eating. Day schools will take care of the children almost from birth. But what about lovemaking, and such perquisites to procreation as a bit of privacy? Will that too be scheduled, by the hour or two, in appointed governmental love-nests? And perhaps most important of all, where will Grandfather Tom and Great-Aunt Bessie go when they no longer feel nimble enough to maintain their own cubicles and their factory jobs? (Dreadful footnote: will they even exist, as family members, once their productive days are over?)

Perhaps this trend toward one-generation living took firm shape only after World War II, when the first monolithic cities rose in dominoes from devastated farmland around places like Paris and Rome. The healthy young women who had survived bombs and invasions married what men were left, and delighted in the elevators and supermarkets and laundromats and day nurseries that had supplanted their childhood days of drawing well-water and knitting socks while they watched the sheep in the meadows. And more than almost anything they loved being free of their mothers-in-law, their demanding parents. Who needed to make room for a dotty old aunt, when the State would take care of new babies? Who wanted a cranky ancestor sitting by the television all day, taking up space at night? Who wanted to take care of them?

It was seldom mentioned in the newspapers, for a decade or so after the "cités" went up, that many dotards jumped from high windows rather than live without a patch of earth to plant, a couple of rabbits to feed. Gradually they disappeared from all the high-rise slums, into discreet hostels as well as their final graves, and by about 1965 it was rare to find anyone sixty-five in the supermarkets. There was no room for them in the high rises. They were a displaced generation, and charitable churches and governments made it cheaper to send them into exile with their peers than to rent space for them with their offspring.

This new way of life, which I honestly believe was an accident of war to begin with, spread fast through Western cultures. In our homeland, who has room any longer to ask Grandfather to come live with his children after his dear wife has died? Who has a nice attic where dotty old Cousin Etta can be gently locked away during the full of the moon? Who has time, anymore, to see that Great-Uncle George's meat is discreetly chopped so that he does not have to take out his clickers and lay them nonchalantly beside his plate at dinner? Above all (and this is the crux of the crux, the secret of the whole sad secret!), who has children who accept not only their necessary parents but their grandparents as an intrinsic part of life?

Until I was almost twelve, my mother's mother was part of all our lives, like hot buttered toast for breakfast and clean hair on Saturdays. It has long amazed and even hurt me that when she died I never felt one pang of sorrow or regret, but only a general relief. By now I understand this, because I doubt that I would ever have loved her, the way I loved my parents and siblings and a few plain human beings. But Grandmother was essential. She shaped all of us, willy-nilly, so that we talked and ate more politely than we might have without her. We spent long good hours with her, while Mother devoted herself to another batch of new babies, and our conversations were full of thought and instruction. When she went off to her many religious convocations, we laughed more at table, and ate more exciting meals than her Nervous Stomach dictated when she was in residence, but when she came back we settled easily again into her decorous patterns. She was there the way books were, or spoons. I don't remember ever kissing her or even feeling her hand, but often I held a skein of new yarn for her while she wound the ball, and then leaned my head against her knees as she read good stories from the Bible. Somewhere there is a picture of my face when I was about four, standing beside her in the stiff folds of her long proper alpaca dress. I look safe and trusting. And I wish that every child alive could be with the detached attention of old people, as I was—live with it as I did.

Grandmother's farthest removed cousins were almost as constant as she, in our house. They came for a month, for the winter, for "a stay." And they expected to be treated with affection and thoughtful dignity, which they always were. Some of them were plainly mad, and one or two were religious fanatics or uplifted birdwatchers or suchlike, but they warmed all of us, and perhaps especially us little people, with their pleasure at being there.

Probably Mother and Father had their moments of exasperation and ennui at this constant flow of Grandmother's peers, but Anne and I loved every minute of it, from dissertations about the significance of every moment of Jesus Christ's Crucifixion to how to make paper furniture for the fairies who, one ancient cousin told us over Grandmother's pious protests, came Midsummer's Eve to a certain rosebush in the backyard.

Yes, housing is to blame. Children and old people and the parents in between should be able to live together, in order to learn how to die with grace, together. And I fear that this is purely utopian fantasy, for a few more centuries perhaps. I am sad that we cannot try again . . . I would have rubbed oil on my grandmother's dry old skin if she had asked me to, and now I would let a child ask to, if there were one nearby. But the course is set, temporarily as History hurtles on, for us to grow up fast, work hard while we are strong, and then die in a premature limbo. I cannot do anything to stop this.

But Sister Age still looks far past us all (Grandmother, little sister Anne, Ursula, her own spoiled brat called something like Johann Wilhelm Sebastian von Ott . . .), and her monkey-sad eyes are brighter than ever, and the letter of information remains open but unread in her bony hand.

Design by David Bullen
Typeset in Mergenthaler Granjon
by Wilsted & Taylor
Printed by Maple-Vail
on acid-free paper